THE JERSEY

We Wear the Mask

By Paul Laurence Dunbar

We wear the mask that grins and lies,
It hides our cheeks and shades our eyes,
This debt we pay to human guile;
With torn and bleeding hearts we smile,
And mouth with myriad subtleties.
Why should the world be over-wise,
In counting all our tears and sighs?
Nay, let them only see us, while
We wear the mask.

We smile, but, 0 great Christ, our cries
To thee from tortured souls arise.
We sing, but oh the clay is vile
Beneath our feet, and long the mile;
But let the world dream otherwise,
We wear the mask!

Alvin Strane

3G Publishing, Inc.
Loganville, Ga 30052
www.3gpublishinginc.com
Phone: 1-888-442-9637

First published by 3G Publishing, Inc. July, 2020

ISBN: 9781941247761

Printed in the United States of America

Contents

Dedication

The Jersey has been a 16 Year labor of Love that two incredible Black Women helped me to birth. Their Love and Encouragement along the way enable me to round the bases.

Moms, Dorothy Strane circa 1932-2013

Becoming a teenage Mom of twin boys at the age of 15 with nothing more than a tenth grade education and eventually having to raise five kids as a single parent the majority of the time while working two jobs, would certainly have placed her in the annals of anybody's Super Mom Hall of Fame. Her challenges didn't stop there. Having to usher the oldest asthmatic twin, that being me, to and from Highland Hospital practically on a weekly basis for her and my treatment visits with Dr. Tuff, little did she realize her life of caregiving had already been set in motion. Her friendship with Bishop Earnestine Reems ignited her passion for the Lord and transformed her from a believer to a true disciple of Christ. Once she picked up the blood stained banner of Jesus Christ her servant leadership of others continued to blossom in children's ministry. Her caregiving skills were put to the test as she nurtured her Mom, Uncle, Father and Sister through their individual health challenges. I'm sure my Mom came to realize that her true calling was caring and nurturing others through sickness and pain. Mom we miss you and thank God for all the Love that you have deposited in all of us Alvin, Albert, Ronald (Pee Wee), Patrice, Samuel (Buttons).... RIP

Lillian Deborah Strane CPA MBA circa 1950-2015

Deborah my bride of 46 Years was a loving Daughter, Sister, Mother and Grandmother who willingly accepted the mantel as the matriarch for both the Robinson and Strane Families after the passing of Mary and Red Robinson and Moms Strane. Her unselfish devotion to family was boundless. While pregnant in her senior year at the University of Oregon she was attending one of her accounting classes when her water broke and Professor Fishcoff offered to escort her over to Sacred Heart hospital on the other side of the campus. Fortunately I was able to rush over with our oldest son Nick to get her to the hospital where she birthed our second son Anrae. Upon graduating from the University of Oregon as the first Black Female to earn a Bachelor Degree in accounting she was hired by Coopers & Lybrand's Portland, Oregon office which at the time was one of the Big 8, CPA firm in the country. Before she reported to her new assignment I was transferred to Los Angeles by Pontiac Division of General Motors, causing her to tell her new employer she would not be accepting the position. The partners at Coopers recognized Deborah's talent and immediately arranged for her to launch her career with Coopers in their Los Angeles office. She actually reported to her new assignment before me and the boys arrived in Los Angeles.

Deborah's enduring commitment to family was ever present as she organized family vacations for our immediate and extended families across the country. Her gift for caring for others was always at the forefront. As an officer in Jack and Jill, Links and her beloved sorority Delta Sigma Theta organization, Deborah's spirit of helping others was ever present. There was no question she was girded in the strength of her Yoakum ancestry.

She chose to endure the constant joggling of her career while holding the family together through 16 relocations across the country during my 32 year career with GM. Her true talent as an executive showed through as she rose to the Vice President level at Parkland Hospital's HMO and Director level positions at both United Health Care and Kaiser Permanent health systems.

The Lord brought Deborah home after a 3 year battle with Breast Cancer. Deborah provided memories that will rest in my heart and in the hearts of all those she touched in her 64 Years on this earth. Sweetheart... RIP

Look for my second Novel entitled "Momma don't take no mess & Thank God for that" where Momma Strane's true story comes to life.

Acknowledgements

To my loving bride, Ramona, who gave me the encouragement to go the distance to bring *The Jersey* to life… I thank profusely. The dedication she exhibited in publishing her first book *Roommates for Retirement* provided me the insight I needed to keep my project moving along.

TJ. White, Genealogist, for allowing me to incorporate his eloquent Postscript that captured the true life and sensibilities that a mixed race slave would have encountered post Emancipation Proclamation.

Constance Williams my first editor in chief. I thank her not only for her editing expertise but just as important for her vivid imagination in bringing the voice of Ms. Hattie to life.

Bert Strane my twin brother for his constant prodding and encouragement as he would say" Man just get it done…Forget the dumb sh.."

Janet and Aaron Talbert for listening intently to my storyline while having breakfast with Ramona and me in Manhattan and saying to me, "You have something, continue to bring your story along". This meant a lot to me because Janet has spent her career as a literary professional for renowned firms such as Doubleday.

Barbara Wilcots for her encouragement early on during the development stage of my storyline. As an author herself her insights were invaluable.

Ozzie Lyles my lifelong friend for his friendship over the years and his eloquent Foreword contribution.

Owerri Marrasha my final editor for her diligence in making *The Jersey* a polished finish product.

Myrna Gale, CEO of 3G Publishing for her professional and caring approach in bringing my labor of Love to fruition.

Cherise Fisher, literary agent and publisher, for her guidance and coaching on impactful scene development.

And most of all I thank my Lord and Savior, Jesus Christ, for all he has done to keep me under his protective wing in a constant state of grace. I have been truly blessed with a life filled with family and friends that have guided me along the way.

PROLOGUE

A Mother's Dream

July 2, 1879

Captain AJ White, Plantation Milner, Georgia

Cap'n had already got up and gone when I rolled over to the other side of the bed. I could still sense his presence. The musty humid air with the douse of his whiskey body odor still lingered in the room. I hear the chirping sounds of the cicadas that eerily remind me of those first days on this here plantation. I was just a frighten little girl, no momma, no poppa in a strange land that spent the better part of her day wallowing in self-pity. I missed my family so much and couldn't stop crying. Cap'n purchase me and two other girls earlier that day at the Savannah slave auction block and brought us here to Milner, Georgia. I remember Molly, one of the older slaves, took us in and clean us up. She was a real blessing for me. She was truly the momma I had lost when my real momma was wrenched from my arms.

That was a long time ago. Today, I gotta clean up this room and go down to help James and Rita with the breakfast chores. Also, I'm lookin for some special mail from my boy today. He up north in that big white school, Brown. All n all, Cap'n ain't so bad as Massa's go. He promised me he would protect our children and he did. I hated to see my boy shipped off up North, but I knew his schooling would keep him out of the cotton fields.

Today is mail drop off day. I am usually able to get my boy's letters before Cap'n looks through his mail. He doesn't mind so much anymore that I read my boy's mail. Things have changed a bit since the Civil War ended a few years back. We's all free now. Lincoln signed that emancipation paper but most of us decided to stay on. Where we gonna go? What we gone do? We still gotta eat. I been with Cap'n now for mor'n 20 years. I done had three of his kids. I fear I'm too old to run off and if I did how would my kids ever find me. My children is scattered. My oldest boy, Bill, look damn near white but he mine. I'm grateful, my boy will never have to pick no cotton. My girls; they up north too. I'll probably never see um again.

Many years ago, my family and I were known as free Negroes in Washington DC. My father had his own business. He was a barber and my mother was a domestic and seamstress. She cleaned white folks' houses and sewed black folks cloths. We had our own home and from what I remember we were happy. Black folks back then were well aware of the slave traders that frequently terrified the Black Communities up North. They would grab free Blacks and sell em down south as slaves. I could remember it like it was yesterday when on a hot summer night when I was 14, two white men busted in the back door of our house waving guns and shouting you Niggers get up and make you way outside and anybody doing any shouting or screaming will be shot right here. Once outside my entire family was tied up at our feet and for good measure our mouths were stuffed with filthy rags and herded into a covered buck wagon outback. We arrived some hours later somewhere south of Virginia Beach where we were transported onto a barge heading south drifting south down the Atlantic coastline. I could hardly bare the pain and fear of what was to come next. My worst nightmare was about to happen when out of nowhere under the cover of darkness this giant ship appeared. Carved into the hull of the ship was the word Clotilda. The sight of this gigantic ship took its toll as I began heave up what little I had left in my stomach. Once on board I was shackled at the ankle to a board that stretched from one end of the ship to the other. There have to have been hundreds of Blacks pinned to the boards in the same manner row after row. The stench and suffocating heat were unbearable. I remember the horrors of that ship as it were yesterday. The nightmare seemed to last forever, though in reality it was only a matter of days before the Clotilda landed at a place called Savannah. Once ashore, we were drugged chained at the ankles onto a stage in front of a ruckus whiskey toting crowd where we awaited our fate. Opening bids for me and three of my fellow shipmates came swift and before I realized what was happening we were carted off and placed in a wagon headed to the Cap's AJ White plantation in Mercer, Georgia.

That was over twenty-two years ago, and I still have nightmares. The only thing that gives me some sense of comfort was the sinking of the Clotilda somewhere off the coast of South Carolina on its return voyage to Africa.

Once downstairs I was greeted by my fellow house servants as Ms. Hattie, the title given me as Cap'n's mistress. I knew they resented my position and saw me simply as the slave who birthed three of Cap'n caramel colored blackies. At eight o'clock that morning, Billy Joe, one of the field slaves brought in the mail satchel. He had retrieved from the postal stagecoach driver at the plantation entrance some two miles away. He carried the satchel to Cap'n office in the front parlor. Among one of my many chores was to sort through the mail and leave them in neat piles on Cap'n desk. I quickly rifled through the mail searching for the one special letter addressed to Captain AJ from Providence, Rhode Island. My son's different writing style made it easy to find his letters. Seeing his unusual handwriting on an envelope, always made my heart skip a beat. When I found one of his letter's I would quickly take it and put it in my undergarments for safe keeping until I had a chance to slip away to my secret hideaway space in the attic of the main house.

I followed Billy Joe to Cap'n's office while chatting light-hearted about the weather. It was a bright, sunny day. One of those that guaranteed long hours of picking cotton. After he put the bag down, I thanked him and immediately began sorting through the mail. He turned to leave the office and told me to have a good day. After a quick scan of today's mail, I quickly determined there weren't any of Bill's special letters addressed to the Cap'n. There was, however, a letter addressed to Captain AJ from Providence, Rhode Island Police Department that caused me to catch my breath. I was afraid to open it because it surely carried bad news. I had no choice, I needed to know if my boy was in trouble and needed help. This had to be about him because his school was in Providence, Rhode Island. Who else from there would write to Cap'n. Bill had completed his third year. What could this letter mean. I decided to take the letter with me. After dinner, once Captain AJ retired to his room with his favorite bottle of whiskey in tow, I made my escape to my secret place in the attic to read the letter from the Providence, Rhode Island Police Department. I lit the candle in the attic and began to frantically tear open the envelope. The letter was from the Providence, Rhode Island Chief of Police Alonzo Patrick. Chief Patrick say he sorry on behalf of the entire Providence Police community. What he sorry about? He say my son been missing from the campus for over ten days and the last time he was seen by anyone was following the Providence Grays baseball game the Saturday before last. Oh Lord, my boy is missing? He says the only thing they found was the enclosed line-up card that reflected his participation in a Major League Baseball game in Providence, Rhode Island on June 21, 1879. What's this all about? To the best of my knowledge my boy only played baseball for the Brown University baseball team. My god, what does this all mean? The absolute feeling of total helplessness was overwhelming. My thoughts quickly shifted as I contemplated how I would approach Cap'n with the news of our son's disappearance. I prayed, "Oh God, take care of my boy wherever he be and return him safely to my arms.

Hattie stayed on her knees at the foot of the bed quite some time crying and praying to God until she finally fell asleep when all of a sudden at dusk the next morning she hears the voice of Cap'n saying "Woman what are you doing down there. Hattie looked up with tears still swelled up in her eyes and starting to crying again as she blurted out "Our boy is missing" Cap'n now fully awake said what do you mean missing. Hattie handed him the Police Captains letter for him to read. Hattie wasn't quite sure how he would take the news. It didn't take long as she observed the usual strong will military officer fall to his knees in a heap sobbing repeatedly mumbling I told that boy to be careful, I told that Boy to be careful. The both of them lie on the floor in a heap at the foot of the bed in complete silence until Hattie blurts out "Well what we gone do. Cap'n didn't hesitate "I will send some of my folks up North and bring that Boy home don't you worry they will find him. Cap'n knew in his heart this incidence may have something to do with Billie's insistence on passing as a white man. Cap'n was quick to remind Hattie that during Billie's search efforts the word may get out that we are seeking information on the disappearance of one of our former slaves and that may have unintended consequences. He shared with her it wasn't uncommon for blood thirsty bounty hunters to join in on the search for slaves thought to be on the run. Hattie said I just want my boy back safely.

Foreword

June 21, 1879, unlike any other hot sweltering summer day in Providence, the sun rose, the birds and bees flew anew, children played, mothers cooked, and dads worked. Some 125 years later what took place in Providence that day captured the attention of Al Strane as he read the article that appeared on the top left column of the front page of the Wall Street Journal on January 30, 2004... Mystery of Baseball: Was William White Game's First Black? As an x-professional baseball player and somewhat of an amateur baseball historian, his first thought was who is this guy William White, and why haven't I heard of him before? Little did he realize the article he read, would start him on a 16-year journey to bring light to what had been relegated to a one line footnote in the official Major League Player Registry. Al's curious inquiry began as a monotonous drip. Drip of factoids that turned into a small stream of intrigue, that ever so slowly grew into a gushing river of mystery and intrigue.

He peels away the layers of greed and power, as the story unravels through the lifelong labyrinth of having to experience life as a brown shoe in a tuxedo world. Is this a sports story, race story, family roots story, who done it story, a love story, or dreams come true story, or perhaps is it simply a tasty bouillabaisse that with each morsel leaves you craving for more.

Jackie Robinson changed the trajectory of baseball, and all professional sports in America forever, when he stepped on the field on April 15, 1947 as the 2nd Baseman for the Brooklyn Dodgers. So, what connects the events of the summer of 1879 to this event? Segregation was the order of the day, MLB, Negro League, Providence, Black, White and until Jackie's debut the only way a person of color could participate in America's pastime was to go undercover, knowing the life left behind would be willingly expunged from their past. The Jersey's depiction of Professional Baseball as the critical driver of wealth, power and greed in this county all while under the auspices of the law, offers up a Win-Win solution to bring about a world that would enable the privileged to get even richer, while at the same time allow the not so privileged to gain a financial foot hold in America's pastime. To the contrary should one find hidden in the abyss, a love story, a love of the game, and a love of a dream, the trip would have been well worth the journey. Fasten your seat belt and enjoy the rollercoaster ride thru the prism of time past, present, and future.

Ozzie Lyles

Oakland Athletics

Training Staff

Chapter 1
Victory Parade

After a two-day train ride from Omaha Nebraska the site of the 1879 College Baseball World Series, the team finally arrived back on campus as the victorious NCAA National Championship baseball team. It appeared the entire student body had come out to celebrate the teams homecoming. The parade route rambled through the quad and down pass the student center and on to the final staging area adjacent to the ball field. If Bill didn't realize before he was now convinced that being a member of Brown University's first collegiate national champion team was pretty special. He noticed in the crowd his girlfriend, Mary McPherson waving her Bill White 1st in our heart banner. The fact that he played first base had something to do with the 1st moniker. As Mary worked her way through the crowd, Bill couldn't help to notice to her immediate left at ten o'clock on the dial was a familiar face, Mary's previous boyfriend, Bobby Trebeck. Bill thought it a bit strange that Bobby would take the time to attend a college baseball team's victory parade. Then it hit him Bobby's presence had more to do with his compulsion to be in close proximity to Mary rather than be a part of the celebration at hand. Bill was sure Mary had no idea Bobby was lurking only a few steps away. Bill's eyes quickly shifted back to Mary as she broke through the crowd and jumped into his arms and laid a big kiss squarely on his lips. Mary and Bill walked the rest of the parade route hand in hand. The experience of being on stage with the rest of his teammates and coaches was pretty awesome. Each player was given the opportunity to acknowledge their appreciation for the support of their fellow players, coaches and fans. When his turn came to take the podium, he couldn't help but think to himself how great it would be to have his Mom share in this awesome experience. But he knew the impact his secret would have on his relationship with his fellow teammates and classmates if they only knew they had accepted the son of a slave master and his mistress into their inter-circle. Bill's persona was always cool and calm on the outside but inside he was hurting. A voice inside always wanting to cry out, "Yea I'm Black, the same person you accepted as your classmate and teammate". He knew exposing his true identity would result in racist reprisals of hatred. Fortunately, Bill was to muffle his inside voice and successfully delivered his address to the exuberant crowd of students and faculty.

As the ceremony drew to a close Bill and Mary discreetly maneuvered their way through the crowd or so they thought. All the while Bobby Trebeck had not let the two of them out of his sight through-out the entire ceremony. The two of them headed down College Hill towards Hope Hall where Mary shared her dorm suite with her suitemate Missy Cornell. Class finals had ended two days prior and Missy and Mary had shared their tear felt goodbyes with one another as Missy prepared to head back to her home in Milford, Connecticut. As they walked through the quad Bill mentioned to Mary, he noticed Bobby perched just behind her in the crowd. At the mere mention of Bobby's name, it was obvious Mary's demeanor took a dramatic turn. She became visibly annoyed and agitated. Bill asked Mary what's the deal with this Bobby guy. She clinched Bill's arm tightly as she grudgingly began to share with him when her and Bobby were dating his behavior had become stifling. She indicated Bobby always had to be the center of attention. It was obvious he thought being a professional baseball player for the Providence Grays Major league baseball club entitled him to treat others as second-class peons. Mary indicated when her and Bobby's brief dating relationship ended Bobby's behavior spiraled out of control. He began to engage in despicable stalking rituals. She went on to say that Bobby's sadistic behavior had begun to exhibit itself in other ways.

Somehow Bobby was able to monitor her daily routine and by doing so he was able to randomly place sleazy provocative notes in her book bag and classroom lockers.

Mary was now starting to hyperventilate when she shared with Bill that Bobby had the audacity to tell her friends and his buddies that their dating relationship had evolved from a purely platonic relationship to a full-blown sexual encounter. As Mary regained her composure, she shared with Bill her last encounter with Bobby was a mid-day face to face confrontation that was witnessed by several of Bobby cronies' right in front of University Hall. She made certain he knew his despicable behavior was deplorable and outright nasty and he needed to get a life. After hearing Mary's heart wrenching description of Bobby's behavior, he knew this guy was a certifiable jerk.

As Bill and Mary approached the back entrance of Hope Hall Mary squeezed Bill's hand and whispered to him that Missy had made her way home for the summer. Mary's pronouncement is what Bill had hoped for from the very first day he met Mary. His baseball and classwork commitments had all but made spending quality time with Mary virtually impossible.

Once inside Mary's dorm room Bill assured Mary, he would be there for her and she didn't have to worry about Bobby any more. Bill wasn't quite sure what that would entail but he was determined to keep an eye out for Bobby. Mary's small modest dorm room was furnished with two beds, two desks and a potbelly wood stove. Mary and Bill settled on her bed and melted into each other's arms. The evening was unforgettable. As Bill awoke the next morning Mary was still asleep snuggled in his arms with a blissful angelic expression on her face. He planted a soft kiss on her forehead and whispered love you… hope to see you tonight. He quickly got dressed and quietly shut the door on his way out and started the quarter mile or so walk back to campus. Still somewhat dusk he couldn't help but notice what appeared to be a male figure lurking in the woods to his left. He kept glancing back to see if what he thought he saw was still there. Whoever it was had disappeared by the time he arrived at the Athletic Director's office where he was scheduled to pick-up his NCAA Championship metal. An envelope with the name Bill White handwritten on the face of the envelope was positioned on the unoccupied reception desk to the right office entrance. When he pick up the envelope he could feel the weight of the championship metal inside but to his surprise in the envelop there was also a box seat ticket to this afternoon's Providence Grays versus the Cleveland Blues Major League Baseball game.

Unbeknownst to Bill as he was picking up his medal at the Athletics Director's office on the opposite side of the campus Bobby Trebeck was making his way down the cobblestone center quad with a non- descript gray tattered burlap satchel in hand heading to the Brown University registrar's office. The walk from one end of the quad to the adminstration building during mid-morning when classes were in session would take a good part of an half hour but now with the majority of the students having returned home for the summer, Bobby was able to move swiftly along to his final destination in a matter of minutes. Once in the registrar's office he placed the satchel on top of the front counter directly in front of the desk on the right side of the room with the nameplate Ms. Lena. On the counter was a small dinner bell that Bobby took it upon himself to pick-up the bell and tinkle it ever so slightly. He first heard the sound of her voice before she appeared from the back office behind what appeared to a multitude of metal safe deposit boxes. Ms. Lena was an attractive middle-aged Native American woman that greeted him with a comforting smile on her face as she arrived at the counter. She asked him what could she do to help him? Bobby introduced himself as Lyle Bradford a student in Nobili Hall. He then began to spend this tale that he had returned to his 4th floor dorm room to retrieve some personal things he had left behind at the end of the semester and he noticed this satchel in the hallway outside of Bill White's dorm room. On a previous occasion Bobby had also followed Bill back to his 4th floor dorm room in Nobili Hall. Bobby posing as Lyle Bradford indicated his dad worked for the postal service and he was confident his dad would be able to see that Bill's satchel was forwarded to him. Ms. Lena knew that Bill White was one of Brown's celebrated baseball players. She told Bobby that she would place the satchel in the storeroom until Bill returned for the fall semester in early September. Anticipating her response, Bobby said that would be fine as he began to slide the satchel closer to her but then he quickly went on to say it appeared the satchel had baseball equipment inside and he knew from previous conversation with Bill that he had planned to play baseball in the summer Cape Cod baseball league during the break. He reassured Ms. Lena, that his Dad would be more than happy to help out. Ms. Lena didn't hesitate and agreed that Bobby's suggestion would be the best and most expeditious way to get Bill his things. She says it would take a moment to pull Bill's student record card in order to retrieve his address. Ms. Lena retraced her steps back to the area where the multiple metal boxes lined the wall. In a matter of moments, she reappeared with what appeared to be a 5X7 index card that was handwritten with Bill White's student information. She placed the card on the counter and then looked for a blank piece of paper and pencil to write down Bill's home address. There happened to be a pencil on the counter but no paper. As she turned around to head to her desk some ten feet away to her left to grab a piece of paper, and left the card on the counter in full view, Bobby was able to gleam from the card blew him away. Fathers Race…. White   Mothers Race… Negro.

Ms. Lena returned to the counter and wrote down Bill's address on one blank sheet of paper and just before she wrote down Bobby's contact information on another sheet of paper for her records she confirmed his name at which Bobby obliged by providing her a factious address for Lyle Bradford. She also scribed on the note the date and the description of the satchel. She handed Bobby the paper and he quickly made his way outside the building. His mind was energized with the thought of how he planned to unload his bombshell discovery to Mary that her boyfriend was a Nigger from a plantation in Georgia.

However, his plan had to be put on pause until after his afternoon ball game between his Providence Grays and the Cleveland Blues.

Chapter 2

Put Me in Coach

Bobby arrived at the ball field around noon two hours prior to the 2:00 PM game time. He went through his normal routine of stretching and tee-hitting drills before he made his way on to the diamond. As he stepped on the top step of the dugout he looked to his left and was stunned to see first baseman, Hank Motters grimacing in pain as he was being helped off the field by two of his teammates. You could see the bone in his right ankle protruding through his blood-soaked stocking. Bobby could barely stomach what he was seeing when he noticed Coach Al waving at a fan in the right field bleachers. The fan leaped down on the field and Bobby couldn't believe what he was seeing. Bobby was blown away when he realized the fan was none other than Bill White himself. Bobby thought to himself what in the hell is this Nigger doing on our field.

Coach Al indicated to Bill that the club was a little shorthanded for today's game and they could use a helping hand, as a result of our first baseman Hank Motter's injury to his left ankle moments ago during pre-game infield practice drills. Bill did not realize what coach meant by help. Helping as a grounds crew member or even better yet as a ball dude to shag foul balls would have suited him just fine. The farthest thing from his mind was the real possibility of competing in a Major League game. Bill was ecstatic when he heard Coach Al say, "Kid this is your lucky day. Head over to the clubhouse and let Moncalm get you suited up. By the way, as an amateur we can only pay you with all the peanuts and hot dogs you can eat." "Coach that's fine with me." Little did they know Bill would have jumped at the opportunity even if he had to pay them to play. Bill's feet never seemed to touch the ground as he made his way to the locker room. Bill was met at the clubhouse door by a stocky colored kid who looked a little young to have a mouth full of chew. The front of his shirt was stained with tobacco chew drippings as he attempted to spit and juggle the chew from one side of his mouth to the other while at the same time uttering sounds that resembled the warbling of a bird. Bill was barely able to discern the kid's questions regarding his uniform and cap size. Moncalm disappeared into the equipment room to retrieve Bill's equipment. To the casual observer, the uniform looked like it had been dragged through the dirt and put away wet, but to Bill it looked as pristine as a freshly pressed sear sucker suit.

As Bill made his way across the diamond Bobby quickly made his way into the outfield to meet up with Coach Al. As he approached Coach Al he blurted out "Hey Coach what's with the kid". Coach Al was quick to say, "Did you see what happen to Hank?". Bobby said yea but what the hell happened …. how did he break his ankle. Coach Al indicated Hank unfortunately got the cleats on his right shoe caught on the first base bag and in doing so his right ankle rolled and his entire body weight came crashing down on his right ankle. So, what's the deal with the kid from Brown. Coach Al asked Bobby if he knew Bill. Bobby was quick to say he knew the kid had played for the Championship Brown University baseball team. Coach Al said the kid is going to give us a hand today by filling in at first base. Bobby couldn't believe what he was hearing. He could hardly contain himself as he turned away and headed back to the dugout. His internal voice was screaming…what in the hell is this world coming too. Not only had he lost Mary his soul mate to a Nigger, but he now had to share his limelight on the diamond with this amateur college kid.

During the game Bill and Bobby chose to distance themselves on and off the field. The rest of the afternoon was a complete blur.

However, when the announcer said, "Now batting for the Providence Grays first baseman Bill White." The entire game experience was so surreal. The final box score would reflect a final win for the Grays but more importantly buried down in the 9th spot in the line-up was first baseman, Bill White 4- 1-1. Translated, 4 at bats 1 hit and 1 RBI. As Bill walked off the field, he realized he had just experienced the mecca milestone of his baseball life. Moncalm met Bill at the clubhouse door with a smile that could have lit up the night skies of all of Providence. "Great job sir". Moncalm told Bill, "Nobody is going to miss that uniform and cap. When you get out of the shower I will have them bagged up for you to take home. Better yet, I would really appreciate your autographing the cap for me." That blew Bill away. He had never signed an autograph, and now Moncalm granted him the ultimate privilege to top off his game time experience of a lifetime. Moncalm handed him a pen and he quickly signed his name to the under bill of the cap. Bill thought to himself, having the uniform as a souvenir was a sweet gift he would cherish forever. Bill jumped in the shower with many of the other ballplayers, after which he got dressed and started on his way home. Right before leaving the clubhouse, clutching his souvenir bag, Coach Al approached Bill to shake his hand. "Kid, super job today. Here's the lineup card from today's game. You can share this one day with your grand kids." "Thanks coach, I can only say it has been an incredible experience. I only wish my folks could have been here to share my joy."

The Grays 5-3 victory was inconsequential to Bobby. His mind was enraged with anger and animosity he felt towards Bill. He wanted to make certain Bill knew his kind wasn't welcomed in his world on or off the field. Unbeknownst to Bill as he left the clubhouse Bobby and three of his red-neck teammates he had just showered with had overheard Bill's conversation with Coach Al. Bobby shared with them the real reason why Bill's folks couldn't have shown up. A mixed-race couple showing up in Providence to support their son would definitely have exposed Bill, who to this point, had lived a seamless Pass'e Blanc existence while at Brown. Bobby wanted to make sure Bill knew there were consequences for his intrusion into his White world. Bobby knew exactly which hot heads to approach to carry out his renegade assault.

As Bill was saying his final goodbyes to Coach Al and Moncalm Bobby and his goon squad readied themselves to depart the clubhouse once Bill departed. Bill waved goodbye and headed off into the night. Within moments after Bill had left the clubhouse Bobby and his crew burst pass Moncalm as they headed in the same direction Bill had taken. They caught up with Bill some two blocks away from the stadium in a back alley a stones throw from the Brown University Campus.

Chapter 3

Ultimate Search Comes to Rest

February 14, 1880

It's been over nine months since Bill's disappearance from Brown University and still no sign of his whereabouts. Cap'n reward of $1000 for any leads to the whereabouts of his missing son has gone unclaimed. This whole ordeal had begun to take its toll on Cap'n mental and physical state. Hattie a fervent prayer warrior had turned to the Lord even more so to give her and Cap'n the strength and comfort to weather the storm. By no means had Hattie given up hope that one day she would see her Billie, but she also realized as the days passed his whereabouts and eventual return was looking more troublesome.

Hattie was going through her normal housekeeping chores in the kitchen when she noticed the monthly mail satchel being placed on the back porch. It was always her hope the very satchel that brought her the horrific news nine months prior would eventually bring her the update that her son was safe and homebound. She retrieved the satchel from the back porch and took it into the front library where she unlatched the clutter pin and poured the mail out on to Cap'n desk. At first glance there appeared to be the usual railroad and plantation business correspondence for Cap'n, but something got her attention. The letter was addressed to Mr. and Mrs. Captain AJ White. This was the first time Hattie had ever seen a piece of mail addressed to Cap'n in this manner. But as she was about to complete stacking mail on the desk for Cap'n review she noticed on one of the envelopes in the return address area a partly smudged word that at first glance appeared to be Prov with all the remaining letters completely erased. Her heart skipped a beat when she realized Prov just might be news from Providence. She quickly pulled the letter and noticed the letter was addressed to Mr. and Mrs. Captain AJ White. Her adrenaline began to spiral out of control because in all her years, she had never seen any such communication addressed to Cap'n that referred to a Mrs. She quickly ripped open the envelop and immediately realized the Mrs., the writer was referring to was actually her.

February 1, 1880

Dear Mr. and Mrs. White:

My name is Mary Blanchard. I am a senior at Brown University. I'm sorry to say it has taken me sometime to be able to locate you. The University and Providence Police department were reluctant to share your contact information while the ongoing police investigation of Billie's disappearance was taking place. I was finally able to convince the University once my baby was born how important it was that I reach out to Billie's parents to let them know they were grandparents of beautiful baby boy named Bill White Jr. in honor of the dad he never met.

Even though Billie and I only knew each other for a short time, I miss him dearly. I can only imagine how devastated you folks are that your son is still missing and unaccounted.

Hopefully in the near future I may have the opportunity to introduce you to your grandson.

Sincerily Yours:

Mary Blanchard 1518 Bordeaux Lane Providence, RI 02912

Hattie's tears were beginning to drip on the letter and wash away some of the print. She was trembling and began to hyperventilate. She ran into the kitchen and immediately her good friend Angie noticed that the usual calm and reserved Hattie was sobbing uncontrollably and grasping for air. Angie said to her, "What's wrong?", and directed her to sit down. While at the same time as Hattie sat down in a chair as she pulled from the cabinet a paper sack and told Hattie to breathe into the sack to help relieve her hyperventilating. It was obvious the letter Hattie was holding was devastating news. As Hattie started to breathe normally and regain her composure, she told Angie she was a Grandma. She said she needed to get with Cap'n to let him know. Angie was shocked because it was her understanding that little Billie was still missing. In light of this development, as shocking as it appeared to be, they may in fact be a step closer to determining the circumstances surrounding Billie's disappearance.

Chapter 4

Peanut Boy

August 1945

Just as Fatty was about ready to fire his final marble into the winning hole he paused ever so slightly to generate a bit more suspense. He heard his Mom's voice, Ms. Josephine to the neighborhood kids, in the distance, starting to penetrate his ear "Bill get in here boy". He knew it was about that time for him to get cleaned up before heading to the ballpark. Both Pound Cake and Pee Wee were relieved to hear Ms. Josephine's call which typically would have brought an abrupt ending to their Holsee marble tournament and their usual ultimate defeat at the hands of the raining marble champ of the Southside Projects. They quickly tried to snatch up their marbles at which Fatty blurted out, "Hold up! You can't do that." Pee Wee didn't hesitate, saying, "You know when your momma calls you bess get your butt back to the house. You know we just trying to help a brother out." They were well aware Fatty's winning marble shot would have cost each of them two of their prized marbles. Fatty snapped back, "Be right there, Mom", while gesturing to his two combatants to hold tight... as to say don't even think I'm going to forfeit this match. With the accuracy of a seasoned archer, he flipped his cat-eye marble and watched it as it trickled down toward the right side of the hole where it landed dead in the center of the final hole. Ball game over! He quickly grabbed up his winnings and tipped his White Sox cap and off he went heading to the house.

Once back home he literally ran through the shower and started to make his way out of the house to the ball park before Ms. Josephine grabbed him by the back of his shirt to make sure he took the time to grab the lunch she had prepared for him which usually consisted of a baloney mustard sandwich and apple from their own one tree orchard in the backyard and an Oreo cookie that he generally would devour first. Momma knew trying to slow Billie down was not in his nature. He had always been a kid that was determined to win at all cost whether that be in their nightly checkers game or marble games with his friends. After she gave him a kiss on the cheek Billie slapped his hand on the framed family heirloom that hung on the wall in the kitchen to the right of the back door as he headed out.

At 12 years old Billie had come to realize Momma took great pride in knowing that Papa's family had passed down what appeared to be some sort of handwritten card no larger than a small postal envelope. When Papa was fatally injured on the job at the local cement factory some six years ago Momma would always say your Dad dreaded going to the plant and not being able to live out his dream of being a big time Negro League team owner. The glass incased frame housed a somewhat faded card that had the printed inscription Providence Grays National League prominently positioned at the top center of the now yellowed card. Under the printed heading was the handwritten date June 21, 1879 and neatly listed below on separate lines hand printed names of nine individuals followed by a number ranging from 1-9. Billie didn't usually pay a lot of attention to Momma's prized possession, but it did puzzle him why the last person on the list, Bill White, would have the number 3 behind his name didn't quite make sense to him. Momma never had much to say about the card but when she did there seem to be a little sadness in her voice and a longing whimsical spirit of how she would have loved to have known her Grandpa.   Little did Bill realize Bill White, his Great Grandpa, was the first mixed race baseball player to play in the Major Leagues. Billie gave his Mom a hug and flung open the back door and off he went.

His first stop was two blocks away from Comiskey Park on the south side of Chicago where he would meet up with Frankie, his peanut supplier. He decided to double his usual order of bootlegged peanuts from 50 bags to a whopping 100 bags in anticipation of the huge crowd expected to attend the annual East-West Negro league All-star game. His official job as an in-stadium peanut vendor was to get his individual sacks of peanuts from the stadium concessionaire, Mr. Foster, that he would sell for 30 cents per bag, earning him 5 cents per bag. But Billie had figured out a way to beat the system by purchasing his peanuts from Frankie for 10 cents outside the stadium and selling them to fans attending the game at the same price of 30 cents per bag enabling him to pocket 20 cents per bag--literally quadrupling his profit margin.

Mr. Foster was always so deep in the suds that he wasn't overly concerned about Billie's apparent lack of his stadium peanut sales. Once in the stadium, Billie couldn't believe the incredible sold out crowd that had come out to join the celebration of the Who's Who in the Negro community. The stadium was rocking. There were as many celebrities in the stands as were on the field. The likes of Cab Calloway, Ella Fitzgerald, Louis Armstrong and even the Champ himself, Joe Louis, were all in attendance. The legendary talent on the field included future Hall of Famers Satchel Paige, Josh Gibson, Cool Papa Bell and a young Jackie Robinson. As Billie hawked his bootlegged peanuts through the crowd, he could only fantasize how incredible it would be for him to one day own a Negro League Team that his Papa dreamed of doing. The thought of having the who's who of celebrities show up at his ballpark gave him an incredible rush. From that day on Billie was determined to make his dream a reality. Unfortunately, for Billie, his dream would have be put on pause because the unintended consequence that resulted from Jackie Robinson's epic signing by the Brooklyn Dodgers Major League and as other Negro League all-stars would join Jackie on Major League rosters, the viability of the Negro League was put to the test. By 1949 in just two short years following Jackie's entry Major League rosters were aggressively adding many of the top Negro ballplayers. Branch Rickey's decision to make Jackie Robinson a member of the 1947

Brooklyn Dodgers started the migration of Negro players from the Negro League to Major League rosters.

The Negro League at that time were the social and economic engines of their respective communities and even though the Negro community, as a whole took great pride in Jackie's accomplishments. The unintended consequence of his accomplishment was the eventual demise of the Negro Leagues.

Chapter 5

Go Jackie Go

April 1947

Boy was it a proud day in the Negro community. Baseball fan or not, the entire country was riveted by the fact that a Black man would be putting on the uniform of a Major League Baseball team for the first time in modern history. The Brooklyn Dodgers now became Black America's team of choice; and wow, did Jackie Robinson show up and show out! What Jackie endured on and off the field was a true testament to his greatness as an athlete but more importantly his staunch display of character would set the tenor for race relations for many years to come. Jackie's success emboldened several other Major League Teams to take the leap. The flood of Black players onto Major League rosters was well underway.

Unfortunately, the unintended consequence of this newfound act of inclusion led to the rapid decline and eventual demise of the Negro Baseball League in America. By the mid-50's, Billie had all but given up on his dream of owning a Negro League. He and his new bride, Dorothy had started their family with the birth of their twin sons, Bill Jr. and Bert. Dorothy, to her credit, had a well grounded sense of family and finances which ultimately enabled both of them to successfully launch their careers. Her nursing career combined with his budding pawnshop business allowed them to live a comfortable middle-class lifestyle in Brooklyn. By the time the boys were 8 years old the Dodgers faithful fans were devastated when their Dodger Bums decided to leave New York and head out West to Los Angeles. Bill could still remember the gut-wrenching conversation he had with his dad 40 years ago when he realized Jackie and the Bums were actually abandoning Brooklyn. The world as Bill knew it had ended. For many years, Bill would tell his boys about his aspirations of owning his own Negro League Baseball Team. Billie's aspiration of owning his own team was embedded in his sub-conscience from the time he hawked bootlegged peanuts as a kid at Cominski. He could remember his dad looking at him, and saying, "I'm going to have my own league". Bill couldn't comprehend how someone, or some bodies could do something so devastating to a community. How could they just take our team and just leave? Dad tried to comfort Bill by sharing with him his thoughts on power, money and greed in the hands of those that use it for personal gain. At a tender age, with a twinkle in his eyes, Bill would say he would one day have lots of money and power and use it to help others and he was going to have his own league and move it wherever he wanted to. Bill would tell his son it was a great idea and encouraged him to follow his dream but always take care of the little people who may not have the money and power but have a desire to be a part of something greater. These are the type of people that will have your back during the hard times. Keep that in mind and you'll be just fine".

Chapter 6

Summer 1982

Three Year Summer

Leon Danford, one of the tournament officials assigned to the Western Regional Oakland Babe Ruth team, arrived at the assigned living quarters of the Oakland, California team compound at the Farmington, New Mexico armory located on the east perimeter of the baseball complex. Initially the facility housed each of the 30 teams participating in the 1982 Babe Ruth World Series. Each team was assigned a designated area that housed their cots within the facility. Once teams were eliminated from the tournament the facility began to empty out. As it now stood, only four teams remained in the armory. Oakland, being one of the remaining teams, hung their banner prominently on the southeast wall of the armory.

Mr. Danford made his way over to the Oakland side of the armory and asked if Billie's Great Grandma, Josephine, had traveled to Farmington with the team? Josephine was surprised to hear her name but without hesitation she said, "here I am." Leon made his way over to her and handed her what appeared to be a Western Union telegram. As she began to read the pale-yellow document you could see her lower lip starting to quiver as tears started to roll down her cheeks. We would find out later the telegram read "Dear Mrs. Williams please be advised your mother, Henrietta Parker, has lapsed into a coma…. We would encourage all family members to expeditiously make their way to Highland Hospital to pay their last respects."

Ms. Henrietta's condition had dramatically deteriorated in the last few days since the team bus departure from Oakland, just over 72 hours earlier. Josephine was well aware that her mom's battle with throat cancer had advanced, but she had no idea it had advanced so quickly and had taken a turn for the worse. Josephine was cautiously optimistic that her mom's condition would stabilize while she attended twin Great Grandsons Billie and Bert's World Series games. Unfortunately, Ms. Henrietta was still struggling to recuperate from her most recent throat surgery when her relapse occurred. Her lifelong addiction to Viceroy Cigarettes, had taken its toll as it now had manifested itself as stage four throat cancer.

Mr. Danford recognized Ms. Josephine's distress and attempted to console her as she wept all the while assuring her that the tournament staff had already put plans in motion to transport her from the Farmington baseball complex to the local Greyhound depot some 20 miles into town. Ms. Josephine asked that her grandsons not be made aware of their great grandma's condition until they completed their game. Mr. Danford promised that her wishes would be honored and off they went in the 1982 Black Chevrolet Bellaire headed to the downtown Farmington, New Mexico's Greyhound Bus depot.

Upon arriving back in Oakland, California at the Greyhound bus terminal some 37 hours later, she was met by a gentleman holding a handmade sign with her name printed on it. He helped her gather her personal affects and ushered her immediately to the awaiting limo and off they went, headed to Highland Hospital. When Josephine arrived at Ms. Henrietta's bedside she still remained in an unresponsive comatose state. Josephine's sister, Gladys, had maintained a constant vigil at their mom's bedside over the last three days, prior to their mom slipping into a coma. Gladys shared with Josephine that the nurse had given her a tin box that Ms. Henrietta brought with her in the ambulance. The nurse told Gladys that Ms. Henrietta wanted to make certain the tin box would be given to her daughters when they arrived at the hospital. Josephine asked Gladys whether or not she had looked to see what was in the box. Gladys responded she wanted to wait to open the box until she arrived. Josephine said, "now is as good a time as any, let's take a look" and with that, Gladys popped open the lid to discover several pieces of jewelry, an insurance policy and an odd looking 4X5 faded yellow card. At the top of the card was printed "Providence Grays Lineup" and right underneath was the penciled in date of June 21, 1879. Right below the date appeared nine individual names with what appeared to be position numbers printed just to the right of each name.

After a quick inspection of the box, they heard the eerie beeping sound coming from one of the many monitors hooked up to their mom. Then within seconds over the sound system they heard "Code Blue, Code Blue, room 415." Immediately, two nurses and the attending doctor on the floor rushed into the room. The nurses ushered Gladys and Josephine out of the room and into the hallway. They could see their mom's bed and the doctor leaning over her aggressively performing CPR. After three to five minutes they watched as the doctor peered into Henrietta's eyes with a light and then re-checked for a pulse and looked at one of the attending nurses and said, "she's gone." He advised the nurse that the time of death was 10:05 PM.

Chapter 7

The Call After The Call

Spring 1984

Two Years Later

Mr. Von Joshua, Sr., current principal at Lowell Junior High School, Oakland ,California received a call from his good friend, George Powles, the current varsity baseball coach at McClymonds High School and regional head talent scout for the Cincinnati Reds. Mr. Powles had built an auspicious reputation for developing young baseball players and bringing them to the attention of the Cincinnati Reds and other Major League teams. Mr. Powles talent pool over the years included such greats as Hall of Famers: Frank Robinson, Willie Stargell and Joe Morgan as well as career major league all-stars, Vada Pinson, Tommy Harper and Curt Flood. After the usual introductory pleasantries, Mr. Powles made an unusual request of his lifelong friend. Von, you have twin brothers, Bill and Bert Williams, enrolled at Lowell. Bill's an eighth grader and his twin brother, Bert, is currently in the ninth grade. I would like to have both these kids attend McClymonds High next year as tenth graders. How can we work this out?

Mr. Joshua was a little annoyed by the request and asked his good friend why was this such a priority. George pointed out that his baseball program at Mack had fallen on hard times and he was confident if the Williams twins joined his baseball program at McClymonds it would bring a much needed lift to his baseball program. Mr. Joshua suggested having both the boys go through a thorough psychological academic evaluation before any decision be made to move forward. Mr. Powles agreed and thanked his good friend for his consideration. Mr. Joshua made it perfectly clear that the decision to move forward to advance Billie from eighth to tenth grade would occur only after the results of the evaluations were analyzed. By March, just two months later, it was determined that Bill's academic and social skills were on par with his twin brother, Bert, and in some academic areas he exceeded his brother's performance. Many years later, Bill and Bert confirmed that they had actually shared the evaluation questions with one another through-out the process.

Needless to say, Bill was excited that he had completed his summer school obligation in flying colors and would be headed off to McClymonds High School with his twin brother as a tenth grader in the fall.

Ms. Dorothy was still winding down from her 40-mile one-way daily work commute to and from the Livermore VA Hospital when she went to retrieve her house phone voice messages. As it turned out she had three missed messages. It was the second message from a Mr. George Baljevich (Mr. B) at St. Elizabeth School that grabbed her full attention. Mr. B indicated St. Elizabeth High School was interested in recruiting Bill and Bert to join their student body. The strange thing was the Williams family were non-Catholic. He asked Ms. Dorothy to return his call or feel free to drop by the school to discuss the school's offer. She decided to wait on mentioning the call to the boys until she paid a personal visit to the one building high school located in East Oakland on 34th Avenue to meet with Mr.B prior to the start of her shift at the Livermore VA hospital. Mr. B was not only the history teacher he also served as the assistant varsity baseball and JV basketball coach. Dorothy was made to feel her boys would be nurtured in a spiritual environment while receiving an excellent educational experience. He walked her through the details of the St. Elizabeth's offer which turned out to be a one full three-year tuition for both her boys. Mr. B was quite convincing and Ms. Dorothy, needless to say, was quite impressed by his offer. She was anxious to discuss this development with the boys but that would have to wait until she returned home from the VA hospital after work.

When she arrived home, she couldn't wait to share what she thought was a life changing opportunity for her boys. Ms. Dorothy was stunned by the reaction she would get from the boys when she shared the St. Elizabeth development with them. She totally underestimated the boys desire to attend West Oakland's McClymonds High School the perennial athletic powerhouse in Northern California. She knew in her heart of hearts, attending St. Elizabeth was an incredible opportunity for the boys. They were quick to remind their mom of all the strings George Powles had pulled to get Bill promoted from the eighth grade to the tenth grade. And not to diminish the fact that they were both excited about the prospect of actually playing high school baseball for George Powles the iconic coach and scout for the Cincinnati Reds. The other elephant in the room was the student-body population at St. Elizabeth happened to be approximately 95% white compared to Mack's Black enrollment which was just the opposite. Needless to say, Ms. Dorothy had the last word and the boys would be headed to St. Elizabeth in the fall.

The boys knew the next assignment was to make the call to coach Powles to explain their mom's decision for them to attend St. Elizabeth High school. Unfortunately, their repeated attempts to get their mom to place the call to coach Powles fell on deaf ears. Bill dialed the number to coach Powles' office and when he answered they both spoke into the handset. Coach Powles was pleased to hear from his new recruits. They went on to share with him their decision to attend St. Elizabeth in the fall but what happened next caught them by complete surprise. Coach Powles was actually elated to hear they had decided to attend St. Elizabeth for two reasons. He felt their Mom's decision was the correct decision for all the right reasons and that they should be mindful of the wisdom she obviously was trying to impart that the education and exposure to other cultures was key for them to experience at this point of their lives. He went on to share with them that by attending St. Elizabeth they would be eligible to join forces with the neighboring Bishop O'Dowd High School baseball team to form what he anticipated would be a powerhouse American Legion baseball team that he would be coaching during the summer.

Coach Powles' prognostication became a reality when two summers later the Bill Erwin American Legion team brought the National Championship to Oakland.

Chapter 8

Brown, Here We Come

The Brown University incoming orientation for the freshman class of 1970 had just begun and Bill was already homesick. This would be the first time in their lives that he and Bert would be apart for any significant period of time. Bill had accepted a full academic scholarship from Brown University located in Providence Rhode Island while his twin brother Bert decided to pursue his baseball aspirations by staying on the west coast to attend Santa Clara University. Needless to say, Bill was a bit apprehensive about his decision to pursue his academic pursuits in public policy and business entrepreneurship. The student ambassador assigned to Bill's group of twenty or so had just been handed their student ID cards and initial class schedules. It was official Bill was now an Ivy Leaguer. Armed with the Brown University Student Conduct Code of Ethics pamphlet along with his meal card and parking pass, for a car he didn't have, rounded out all the paraphernalia he would need to navigate through his first year at Brown. It didn't take him long to begin to put his entrepreneurial talents to work. He figured the parking pass he had in his procession was of no value to him, in light of the fact he didn't own a car but for a fellow commuter student this parking pass was worth $50 for the semester. He had already devised a plan that would generate an additional revenue stream by leasing out the use of his parking pass to some unsuspecting upperclassman. He had already begun his unofficial entrepreneurial training.

Bill refocused his thoughts to the task at hand as he followed the ambassador and his fellow classmates as they made their way through the campus grounds wondering how much longer the orientation would drag on before he'd have an opportunity to grab lunch. The jock assigned to escort his group didn't seem overly enamored with his role as their headmaster for the day. Bill got the sense that the only reason someone would take on this ambassador gig is because they were desperate for extra cash.

Finally, as the group started to make their way to the cafeteria located in the student union they passed through the athletic promenade where the banners and photos of current and past Brown University athletic teams were on display. Something caught Bill's eye as the group whisked past the 1879 Brown University Baseball Intercollegiate National Championship team photo display. It wasn't just the photo's vintage gray uniform, gloves and bats but just to the right of the coach sat a player whose complexion appeared to be of a slightly darker hue than the rest of his teammates. Bill initially thought to himself maybe because the photo was almost a 100 years old the discoloration may have attributed to the disparity, but he quickly changed his perspective when he realized if anything, the fading black and white print would have made all the players lighter not darker. He thought to himself could it be that there may have been a Black kid back then a Negro kid playing baseball at Brown University back in the late 1800's. His pre-occupation with the photo lingered on while the rest of his classmates continued on the orientation tour heading to lunch. Bill's audible hunger pains had totally disappeared as he reflected on the prospect that there may have been a brother who played at Brown back then. He thought to himself that would be a hell of a story to share with his brother Bert. He took a closer look at the handwritten caption underneath the photo where it displayed the names of the individuals in the photo and he found the name of the player in question was Bill White.

As he hurried to catch up with his group, he couldn't stop thinking about who was this guy, Bill White.

That night, Bill was on the phone with Bert recapping his uneventful orientation day at Brown. At the end of the call Billie causally mentioned the photo that caught his attention. Bert was quick to say he seriously doubted a Black kid played for Brown's only National Championship Intercollegiate team. Bert's skepticism only fueled Billie's curiosity even more. He was committed to do some more digging to find out who was this Bill White guy. Billie knew it would have been a anomaly to have a Black male attend an Ivy League college up north back in the late 1800's. However his limited knowledge of Black History did indicate, although rare, there were recorded instances where White slave owners would bank roll the college education up north of their fair skin mixed race kids fathered with their Black mistresses. These kids would enroll as White students leaving behind any connection to their mixed heritage.

Bill always had more than a passing interest in how Blacks in the 1800's were able to succeed with all the obstacles confronting them in gaining access to highest levels of education offered by the premiere institutions of higher education. Bill knew he had to find out if Bill White could have been one of those unknown Blacks who was forced to live a double life in order to be able to take advantage of a privilege that his White counterparts viewed as their God given right.

Chapter 9
The Cap

Bill's freshman year experience at Brown was coming along in typical fashion--all-nighters followed by Friday night dorm keg parties and classroom lectures that never seemed to stop. But all in all, no surprises. However, the haunting thought regarding the 1879 Brown Baseball Team photo and Bill White the player was ever present in his sub-conscience. He decided to continue what had now become an obsession to keep digging to determine Bill White's background information. He first approached the athletic department only to find out all student files were preserved at the registrar's office. That being the case, Bill's next stop was at the registrar's office where for some reason when he mentioned student files going back specifically to 1879, he was directed to the office of the President. Bill was starting to feel for whatever reason these archive files no longer existed or at best if they did exist, they were sealed and unavailable for public viewing. As he arrived at the President's office, he was met by Sylvia Swinehart administrative assistant to the Vice Provost of Student Affairs, Ms. Barbara Gary.

Bill explained to Ms. Swinehart his interest in wanting to discover the identity of Bill White, a member of the Brown University 1879 National Championship baseball team. Ms. Swinehart asked Bill to have a seat while she attempted to contact Ms. Gary. About five minutes had passed when Bill was told that Ms. Gary was available, and she directed him to the office at the rear of the corridor. Ms.

Gary met him at the door and asked him to have a seat in one of the chairs facing her desk. She asked him how she could be of assistance. Bill went on to tell her why he had taken such an interest in a player featured in the team photo positioned in the athletic center of the 1879 Brown University NCAA National Championship baseball team. The meeting all of a sudden took an awkward turn when he mentioned Bill White as the person of interest. Ms. Gary appeared stunned that Bill would have an interest in a photo over 120 years old. Unbeknownst to Bill, Bill White's name was associated with one of the darkest moments in Brown University stoic history. Ms. Gary was well aware of Mr. White's disappearance and the apparent cover up. She shared with Bill that Brown University back in the mid 1800's had welcomed mulatto mixed race students from well-to-do White Southern families into their student population with the understanding that the University, under a vail of secrecy, would categorize those students as being White on all University enrollment paperwork. She knew this policy was more for the protection of the school's endowment initiative than for the protection of the student's anonymity. In many cases the enrollment applications of these southern Mulatto students were accompanied by a sizable endowment commitment to the University. The University had become complicit in the arrangement to the point they would solicit such students in their recruitment efforts.

Ms. Gray went on to share with Bill that the University was rumored to have direct ties to the vibrant Providence slave trade auction houses. Only recently had the University officially acknowledged the fact that several of its board of governors just happened to be slave ship owners. The University had repeatedly denied they were active participants in the actual brokering of slaves throughout the southeast corridor of the United States. However, Brown did admit they were being financially compensated for serving as an intermediary between the slave traders and the ship owners. Ms. Gary went on to say the official school accounts indicated that when the White family approached the University after their son's disappearance the University took on a special interest in the case because Captain AJ White had been a prolific purchaser of slaves through the Providence slave auctions in an effort to supply the manpower needed to expand his growing railroad interest throughout Georgia. The records indicated Bill White was one of the many southern Mulatto students that were enrolled as being White. Needless to say, Bill was stunned by what he had just heard. Once he regained his composure, he asked Mrs. Gary was there a thorough investigation done by the authorities at the time regarding Bill White's disappearance. It was her understanding the local authorities were in communication with the University and the family throughout the year-long investigation.

The official police reports indicated Bill White had played in a 1879 mid-season game for the Providence Grays of the National League. The game was played at the then Olneyville neighborhood stadium which was no more than five miles from campus. Mr. White was never seen or heard from again after leaving the stadium following the game. The entire University student body engaged in the search but to no avail. Apparently according to the police account the only thing that was recovered was some sort of lineup card and what was thought to be his baseball glove. The final investigation report indicated both items were returned to the White family. Bill was still reeling from what he had just heard when he asked Mrs. Gary if she knew if anyone still associated with the University who may have any additional information regarding Mr. White's disappearance. She thought that was highly unlikely since anyone from that time frame would now be close to 100 years of age.

Bill thanked Mrs. Gary for being so open in sharing this part of Brown's history. As a woman of Color, he could tell she was visibly touched. She went on to say it wasn't uncommon for Slave bounty hunters to travel up North to kidnap their victims. In Mr. White's case, we just don't know what led to his disappearance. Slave bounty hunters were known to travel up north to kidnap their victims. As Bill departed Mrs. Gary's office, he had come to the realization that his efforts to resolve the mystery of his 1879 baseball player had come to a dead end. However, not one to give up easily he wondered to himself whether or not there was something he missed or perhaps something he overlooked. He decided to go back to the beginning and that meant heading back to the athletic promenade to take a closer look at the team photo. When he arrived at the promenade, he studied the photo in greater detail and realized there was a young kid in the photo who appeared to be the batboy. He thought to himself just maybe this kid, who would be in his mid-nineties, might still be alive. He quickly took out his iPhone 5 and snapped a photo and forwarded it to Mrs. Gary with the caption "any idea who the kid is in the photo?" She immediately knew the kid in the photo was Moncalm Robinson, the 50-year retired Brown University maintenance supervisor. It was a well-known fact at the University that Moncalm had been associated with the University in one capacity or another for over 90 Years. When Bill looked at her response and realized this may be the breakthrough he was hoping for. He immediately searched Google's 411 directories where he found a listing for a Moncalm Robinson at 323 Sterling Drive, Providence, Rhode Island. Bill decided first thing after class the next day he would pay a visit to Mr. Robinson's home.

At 3:20 PM, the next afternoon, Bill stepped on the front stoop of 323 Sterling Drive and rang the doorbell. After two rings the door opened and behind the screen door was a strikingly attractive young lady who he would find out later was Mr. Robinson's Great Granddaughter, Dorthey, who was a second-year law student at Brown. She asked if she could help him. Bill introduced himself and asked if Mr. Robinson would be available to talk with him. She asked him what his interest was in wanting to meet her great Grandpa. He told her he wanted to know if Mr. Robinson could remember anything regarding the disappearance of Bill White back in 1879 after playing in a game for the Providence Grays Baseball team. She tells Bill that unfortunately her great Grandpa suffers from dementia and today might not be the best day to meet him. Bill asked if he could just come in to introduce himself. She thought for a second and then said, "ok just for a moment." She unlocked the screen door to let him in. Bill entered the foyer and she led him into the family room where he noticed this frail old man sitting up in a Lazy-Boy recliner with a light blanket wrapped over his legs. His great granddaughter introduced Bill as a student from Brown who wanted to ask him if he remembered a Bill White from his days with the Grays.

It wasn't apparent by Mr. Robinson's reaction that he even heard his great granddaughter's introduction of Bill. Suddenly Mr. Robinson appeared to sit up in his Lazy Boy and gestured to his great granddaughter for a bottle of water. And after a small sip of water he cleared his throat and blurted out "the Cap the Cap." His great granddaughter noticed how agitated her great grandfather was becoming and she asked him "great Grandpa, what do you mean?" He began to point to the China cabinet in the adjacent living room. His great granddaughter made her way over to the China cabinet and looked inside the glass doors and noticed on the top right-side shelf a gray baseball cap with a "P" on the front panel of the cap. She reached in the cabinet and pulled the cap off the shelf and handed it to her great Grandpa.

Both Dorthey and Bill immediately noticed a change in Mr. Robinson's body language and also what appeared to be a slight twinkle in his eyes. His posture was more erect and his voice tonality left nothing to the imagination when he began to share his memory of Bill White, "That boy was something. He came right out the stands, and I suited him up. I can remember it like it was yesterday. He even got one hit in the game. After the game, I asked him if he would autograph this here cap for me; and see, pointing to the under-bill of the cap, here's his autograph. He was so excited and then he told me and the coach the only thing missing from his incredible experience was having his folks watch him play. I did notice several of the red-neck players who he had just showered with seem to be taking special interest in the kid's eventual departure from the clubhouse. When he went to hand me his uniform I told him to keep it being it was the last game before the mid-season break. The skipper also handed him the line-up card from the game and off he went. I should've known something wasn't quite right when I saw those red-neck players rush out of the clubhouse in hot pursuit of the young fellow." Bill could see tears welling up in Mr. Robinson's eyes as he eased back in his Lazy Boy. As Mr. Robinson's mental acuity level seemed to decline, Bill quickly asked him, "Did the authorities approach you for information regarding the player's disappearance?" Mr. Robinson buried his face in his hand and said, "I was only a kid, and I was afraid to say anything fearing something bad might happen to me."

His great grand-daughter said, "I think Grandpa is a little exhausted. Maybe you can come back another time." Bill said he understood and thanked Mr. Robinson, who now appeared to be sobbing openly, for being so gracious with his time. Bill indicated he would show himself out. As Bill made his way back to campus, he realized foul play at the hands of Bill White's own red neck teammates and not slave traders were at the root of his disappearance.

Bill realized his search for truth surrounding Bill White's disappearance had reached an unceremonious conclusion.

Chapter 10

Barnstorming

August 1, 2010

After nine months it was apparent Bill's attempts to schedule a meeting with Major League Baseball (MLB) to discuss his barnstorming proposal was going nowhere. He had but given up hope that his lifelong passion to make an impact on the big stage of professional baseball would never see the light of day when for no apparent reason Bill received an email alert from MLB requesting he contact them at his earliest convenience to arrange an appointment to meet with their competition committee board members. Bill couldn't believe his eyes, perhaps because they were beginning to tear up, but he managed to regain his composure as he yelled out to his brother in the adjacent office, "Bert we are in." Bert vaulted over to Bill's office. "In where?" Bill enthusiastically pointed to his computer monitor as he reversed the screen for Bert's review. When Bert saw the subject line of the email which read "MLB Meeting Request" he too began to get emotional. He knew how much this meant to his brother and the entire organization that had put so much time and energy into developing the barnstorming initiative.

Ever since Bill started his sports marketing firm five years earlier, his focus has been on becoming a part of the massive partnership network of Major League Baseball (MLB), which has been dominated by Majority-owned marketing firms. Bill viewed MLB as a bastion of a privileged society that had denied Minority-owned marketing firms the opportunity to get part of the game action. Barnstorming became the only option, years ago, for minority ownership and players to compete on a grand scale. He recalled from the book Satchel: The Life and Times of an American Legend by Larry Tye, "Barnstorming brought baseball's icons to small towns with no stoplights but lots of barns, and it gave hamlet heroes at least the fantasy that they might someday be discovered."

The whole barnstorming notion came about around the time his brother Bert joined the firm. Bert had followed in the footsteps of their dad Bill Sr., who himself, had toiled in the minor leagues nearly 30 years ago during the late 1970's. Bert's professional baseball career was a hopscotch of stents in the minor leagues where he competed in the United States, Mexico and Puerto Rico. When Bert shared with Bill his experience of playing in the different leagues, it reminded him of an article he read regarding the barnstorming team Satchel Paige pulled together for Dominican Republic dictator, Rafael Trujillo (El Jefe), for the 1937 Dominican World Championship. Satchel's team successfully captured the championship. When interviewed sometime later, Satchel indicated that the dictator had invited his barnstorming team back the following year. Satchel was quick to decline the invitation as a result of Trujillo's suspected genocide activates within his own country.

Bill then said to Bert, "In light of what's happening now with the 18-month labor dispute between the owners and players, what if we pulled together our own barnstorming tour of major league players?" Bert responded, "This could be quite timely". Bill said, "This might be the entry point we've been in search of to gain a foothold into the MLB partnership network."

Bill would later discover the impetus to move the barnstorming presentation forward was the result of impending negotiations between key owners and the player's union that had reached an impasse. Players who were to be free agents were now being told due to the strike they would not be arbitration eligible for the upcoming season unless the protracted strike were to end by the start of spring training. Somehow the media got wind of the barnstorming proposal and immediately began to publicize it as a credible solution in bringing the owners and the player's union back to the bargaining table and the eventual return of Major League Baseball after a year-long Owner/Player dispute. During the strike year, public opinion had hardened against both owners and players. The hope of seeing some sort of barnstorming tour appeared to ignite fan enthusiasm that baseball would soon be back on the field. Bill was confident the barnstorming initiative would go a long way in improving the tarnished public persona of both the owners and the players. He also knew the passive revenue streams that would be generated from a barnstorming tour would benefit the coffers of both owners and players. Bill was able to secure his meeting with the MLB executive competition committee the following week.

Upon arriving at the MLB offices, located at 245 Park Avenue, Manhattan, New York the security guards put Bill through MLB's security protocol. His photo was taken and embossed on an ID badge. What he didn't realize was his photo was electronically forwarded to the fifth-floor executive offices where he was scheduled to meet with the executive competition committee. With his newly imprinted pictured badge attached to his sport coat breast pocket, he waited anxiously at the elevator for his escort. He was stunned when the elevator door opened and off stepped Ms. Deborah Robinson a gorgeous, sophisticated woman dressed in a stunning black St. John knee length suit that only enhanced her beauty. You could tell by Bill's initial reaction he was stunned to see MLB had such a gorgeous sister as their Chief Legal Counsel. After his momentary lapse Bill regrouped and refocused his attention on the task at hand. After they exchanged pleasantries they got on to the elevator heading up to the 6th floor. As Deborah slid her badge into the elevator security slot to activate the button for the 6th floor she was thinking to herself … this brother is fine. She quickly redirected her focus as they exited the elevator to make their way to the Commissioner's conference

room where Bill was scheduled to meet with the MLB Competition committee.

As Deborah escorted Bill into a conference room where already seated were the Wall Street looking white guys who appeared to be hunting for fresh meat to devour. Deborah opened the meeting by introducing Bill and stating that the purpose of the meeting was to review Bill's barnstorming initiative. She immediately turned the meeting over to Bill. Bill was quick to describe himself as a devout baseball fan who wanted to see the current labor dispute end sooner than later. In the interim, however, his interest was to bring baseball back to the fans by initiating an independent barnstorming exhibition series to take place in the Arizona and Florida corridor during the fall and winter timeframe. It was obvious Jake Everhardt, Vice Commissioner, soon to be appointed as the new Commissioner, was powerbroker of the assembled panel. After Bill concluded his presentation. Jake started the barrage of questions by asking why MLB should endorse this barnstorming initiative. Bill provided what he thought were insightful ideas on what the MLB owners and active players stood to gain by undertaking the barnstorming proposal. Bill pointed out his proposal was a true Win-Win proposition for all the stakeholders: owners, players and fans. Win for the players monetarily, emotionally and physically. Win for the team owners monetarily and public relations. Win for the fans desire to see their beloved players back in action.

Most of the questions offered up from the group were fairly mundane and disingenuous in nature with the exception of Ms. Deborah, MLB Chief Legal Counsel, who drilled down to the issue of indemnification and the use of MLB properties to promote the barnstorming tour. Bill assured the group his attorneys would provide the MLB with all the necessary contractual documentation to address their concerns regarding indemnification and the use of MLB properties in promoting the tour. Bill couldn't help but notice Jake Eberhard's body language when Ms. Deborah attempted to address the issues she felt were germane to the topic being discussed. His condescending behavior toward Ms. Deborah was not only distracting but out right vulgar. As the meeting drew to a close, Jake regained some sense of civility as he thanked everyone for taking time away from their busy schedules, and also acknowledged Bill for his creative barnstorming approach. He advised Bill that his committee would have further discussions and would make the determination whether or not his barnstorming proposal would be granted further consideration at the MLB Executive Committee level. As he prepared to depart the room, he couldn't help but reflect on the charade he had just experienced. Even more discouraging was the thought that the future leadership of MLB would be spearheaded by a jerk like Jake Everhardt.

Ms. Deborah rose to escort Bill back to the lobby. They walked down the corridor past a glass encased office exquisitely decorated with an adjoining conference room. Bill's eyes were drawn to a plex-i-glass cube frame with a dingy faded gray baseball jersey with a prominent "G" positioned on the left breast area. Deborah noticed his gaze and pointed out that this was Vice Commissioner Jake Everhardt's office. Bill thought to himself, "Nice digs." But there was something else he felt in his gut, but he couldn't put his finger on it at the time.

Once back in the lobby Bill mustered the courage to ask Deborah if they could get together again. She was quick to say contact her secretary for an appointment. Bill quickly explained his hope was to get together after hours for a drink. She thought for a moment and said "ok. Call me tomorrow," and she gave him her mobile number.

As Bill made his way back to Grand Central, he thought to himself even though the meeting hadn't gone as he had hoped he was excited about the prospect of spending some time with Ms. Robinson.

Chapter 11

Dead on Arrival

8:07 AM Monday, February 14, 2016 Bill's caller ID lit up indicating an incoming call from Deborah. With cat like reflexes Bill was able to answer the call before the end of the first ring tone. Bill knew right away when Deborah addressed him as Mr. White that the call was strictly business. Regardless just hearing her voice was a welcomed surprise. As she abruptly introduced herself, she went on to advise him that he would be receiving an official letter from MLB indicating his proposal to conduct a series of barnstorming tournaments had been rejected by the MLB Executive Competition committee. Needless to say, her pronouncement didn't come as a complete surprise especially in light of the fact that it had taken over nine months to get an audience with the MLB powerhouse team.

While Bill was still miring in his disappointment, the mood of the call seemed to make a complete flip-flop when Deborah said, "Mr. White why don't we meet for lunch to discuss potential venues within MLB that may present viable partnership opportunities going forward." Even though the meeting hadn't gone as he hoped Bill was excited about the prospect of spending time with Ms. Robinson in the near future.

Once arriving at the restaurant, which was a step down below street level at the intersection of Houston and Canal Street, Bill was struck by the luxurious appearance of rich nautical décor, one could imagine exists on luxurious yachts, definitely not your typical lunch meet and greet location. The thought occurred to him why would Deborah select this particular restaurant, which was located at the foot of Manhattan Island several miles away from the 245 Park Avenue MLB headquarters.

Deborah arrived shortly after 12 noon and they were escorted to a table closest to the rear of the restaurant where she positioned herself with her back facing the front entrance of the restaurant. The restaurant site selection and our seating arrangement all appeared to be somewhat clandestine. Bill thought to himself; imagine sitting at the rear of a restaurant that sits below ground level, the likelihood of one being seen from the street would be slim to none.

Bill soon realized this entire meeting and location was a calculated risk on Deborah's part. Apparently, she had something she wanted to share with Bill that would change their relationship forever. After exchanging the usual pleasantries, she made Bill aware that his barnstorming proposal was "Dead on Arrival" for the simple reason he was not part of the "Good old boys" network the MLB relied upon to conduct their normal business affairs. She also pointed out that the only reason he was granted an audience at MLB was the result of the pressure the Players Union had exerted on MLB to break the stalemate between players and owners' contract talks. Over the last nine months with no realistic end in sight both parties had reached a point of no return. Deborah could see the dejected look on Bill's face. He felt like he had been sucker-punched. Bill thought to himself, "It never fails, the rich and powerful always seem to figure out a way to hold on to theirs at all cost, protecting their own self-interests. Unfortunately, outliers like him have to constantly battle to get their fair share of the pie or at least a few crumbs that fall off the table. Bill was reminded of his dad's aspiration of owning his own Negro League Team. Bill had seen enough over the years and was fed up with the notion that the inside powerbrokers called all the shots and everyone else had to rely on benevolence of the powerbrokers. The old crab in a barrel phenomenon comes to mind, which always ends up being a Win-Lose trade-off for the little guy. Bill was determined to be the outlier who would beat the MLB establishment at their own game.

Deborah sensed Bill's frustration and, in an attempt to pull him up from the depths of his frustration, she offered him what she considered to be an olive branch. Bill felt her gesture was more like a Redwood tree. She went on to share with him her insight into the inner workings of the MLB establishment. She simply encouraged him to follow the money. It's not by accident that these owners were extremely wealthy people who knew how to capitalize on their investments by using other people's money to strengthen their investments. Then she asked Bill if he had considered offering the players and their agents the ability to participate in traditional Spring Training regimens at sites in both Florida and Arizona? His firm could orchestrate all the logistics, including but not limited to providing the sites, coaches, trainers, and nutritionists.

Bill was now starting to fill in the blanks. He realized this approach would allow his team to develop a revenue stream for not only the players and coaches but also the trainers; none of whom were being paid during what was now approaching the ninth month of the bitter long labor dispute between the owners and players. Deborah's recommendation blew him away. Deborah may have thought she was extending him an olive branch to make up for the humiliation that MLB had put him through, but Bill saw it for what it was, Deborah had planted a giant Redwood tree in his front yard. Bill knew this type of initiative could catapult the credibility of his firm in the eyes of the baseball community. MLB's blessing would go a long way in gaining the approval of the players union and coaches. Bill's adrenaline was starting to ramp up with the thought of pulling together his team to make this Spring training idea a reality. Deborah could tell Bill was totally on board. Bill knew getting the player agents to buy–in would be the challenge. But he also knew he had an ace in the hole he could count on to run interference with the top baseball agents in the industry. His lifelong homeboy, Ozzie Terry, just happened to be one of the top sports agents in the industry who happens to be the International Management Group, IMG, Sports

Academy Chief Operating Officer. Bill realized the only way he was going to gain the conditional acceptance of MLB and the owners would be to appeal to their greed and ego by enabling them to soak up all the public accolades and social media hype that would surely be generated by the training site proposal.

Deborah finished off her seafood pates while Bill inhaled the final morsels of his crawfish ettoufe'. They concluded their lunch engagement with Bill indicating he would have a formal proposal ready to present to the MLB Competition Committee within the month. He asked if he could count on her support to help position him for a second audience at MLB to present his proposal. She said she would do what she could but it was on him to return to MLB in a timely fashion with a proposal that would meet the needs of all the stakeholders, MLB, Owners, Agents, Players and Coaches.

Bill escorted Deborah to the front door of the restaurant where her Uber car awaited her. He thanked her for the opportunity to have lunch and her invaluable insights. As she entered the back seat of her Uber car Bill planted a gentle kiss on her left cheek that took her somewhat by surprise. As her ride headed off uptown back to her office on the Upper East Side, she realized Bill had feelings for her and the feelings were mutual. Bill's mind was racing with the thought that he had an incredible lunch with a beautiful lady that threw him the lifeline he had been seeking for years. He thought to himself… Well you wanted to play in the big boys' sand box, here's your opportunity. He hailed down a taxi and hit speed dial to call Ozzie Terry.

Chapter 12

Me Too

Bill received an unexpected call from Deborah at about 4 PM the Monday following their Friday lunch date. Her tone and the immediacy of her request caught him off guard. She asked if they could meet for dinner that evening at Victor's café, an intimate Cuban restaurant at the corner of 52nd and Broadway, her treat. Without hesitation Bill asked what time worked best for her. She said she would make the reservation for 6 PM.

Bill arrived early, at approximately 5:45 PM, and settled in at the bar. At about 6:15 PM he peeked out the bar window overlooking 52nd street and noticed Deborah climbing down from the carriage seat of her peddle powered rickshaw. The operator was quick to shelter her from the driving rainstorm with his oversized umbrella. Once inside the restaurant foyer Bill helped Deborah remove her rain drenched Burberry trench coat. Bill couldn't help himself as he asked Deborah why the open-air rickshaw and not the more traditional taxi mode of transportation. If looks could kill…. Deborah with no hesitation bluntly asked Bill when was the last time he tried to hail a taxi during rush hour outside of Grand Central on a rainy night. Before Bill continued his subtle line of questioning, he could sense something was not quite right.

Deborah's demeanor which was usually quite composed and upbeat was now quite stoic and strained which was totally out of character for her. Bill took a more conciliatory approach when he asked her what was wrong. Deborah took a deep sigh as she excused herself and headed off to the ladies' room. Upon her return the maître d' escorted them to their booth which was located in the rear of the colorfully decorated Cuban open-air venue restaurant. Bill could tell something was not quite right. He asked how her day had gone. What happened next was totally unexpected. Deborah started sobbing profusely as she buried her head in her table napkin. Bill slid over in the booth and placed his arm around her shoulder. Bill asked her, "What's going on?" She paused momentarily and wiped the tears from her eyes and cheeks and mumbled an inaudible series of words that sounded like "that asshole Jake." She then cleared her throat and went on to share with Bill the horror that had punctuated her day.

Deborah described what started around noon when she received a call from the vice commissioner's secretary, Lynn, to report to Jake's office at my earliest convenience. After completing an email document, I hastily grabbed my phone and headed over to Jake's office which was on the opposite side of the sixth-floor atrium of the MLB headquarter building. Upon entering the vice commissioner's outer office, which was located just to the right of the junior executive conference room, Lynn while still on the phone, waved for me to proceed into Jake's office. Once inside, Jake acknowledged my arrival and tells me he wanted me to join him at a client luncheon meeting downtown. He directed me to grab my things and meet him in five minutes at the rear executive elevator. As I headed back to my office to grab my purse, I shoved my phone in my coat pocket and headed toward the rear elevator. As I headed down the hallway, I thought to myself; why would we be using the rear elevators which led out to the street level of the executive parking structure located at the rear of the building.

Generally, when attending client luncheon engagements in the city we would grab a taxi to make our way around town. I didn't give it much more thought as I made my way to the elevator. As I approached the elevator, I could see Jake had already positioned himself at the entrance. Once in the elevator Jake positioned himself at the front side of the elevator where the floor control panel was located. He was sporting his usual gray cashmere overcoat. All of a sudden without me noticing, Jake reached back with his right hand and in one swift motion he punched the red stop button and the elevator came to a screeching halt somewhere between floors 5 and 4. My initial reaction was that there was some sort of electrical failure, but to my amazement, Jake had unbuckled his belt and dropped his trousers to the floor exposing his completely naked lower torso. It all happen in a matter of milliseconds. My fight or flight instincts kicked in immediately. I reached for my right foot three-inch stiletto pump and told him if he came any closer, I would plant that heel right in his crotch. His smug response was sickening. He had the audacity to say he saw me with my brown sugar boyfriend last week and he just wanted me to know his white meat could satisfy my every need.

At first Bill was stunned by what he was hearing but his emotions quickly changed to rage. Hearing Deborah's story reverberated Bill's anger on multiple fronts. Jake's despicable behavior had deeply traumatized someone he deeply cared for, and secondly his racially charged comments regarding his sexual superiority enraged Bill to say, "This asshole has got to go." Jake's putrid display of entitlement harkened back to the to the plantation mentality that characterized Whites as the privileged race and Blacks as something less than human.

Bill asked Deborah, who was still visibly shaken, if there was anything he could do. She indicated she hadn't determined what her next move was going to be, but she assured Bill whatever she decided to do Jake would know he messed with the wrong person and he would pay dearly for his actions. But for right now she said she would like nothing more than a stiff drink and some good Cuban food. Bill called their waiter over, ordered a double Jack and coke on the rocks for them both. Following dinner, Bill escorted Deborah out to her Uber ride that was waiting out front. Bill asked Deborah if she would allow him to drive her home, but she declined politely by saying not tonight but let's talk tomorrow. Bill gave her a soaking hug as she melted into his arms. As she was about to climb into her ride Bill knew she was the one he had waited for all his life. At 6 AM the next morning Bill's phone messenger alert started flashing incessantly followed by a multitude of hand clapping emoji's messages saying, "Thank You".

Little did Bill know Deborah had already developed a plan to take down Jake and put MLB squarely on notice that sexual harassment was unacceptable and would not go unchallenged. Her immediate challenge was to secure the elevator camera feed from the executive elevator. She knew the video feed would clearly show the despicable behavior of her boss. Having the video in hand would give her all the ammunition she needed to attack Jake's credibility. Her plan was to pay a visit to the security staff office by 8:30 AM to secure the previous day's recording. The security office was located at the rear of the front lobby.

As she arrived at the security office the Chief of Security was about to depart his office. She noticed he appeared to have a CD cradled in his left hand. She asked if she might speak with him a minute. He told her he had to deliver something to the Vice Commissioner's office and when he returned, he'd be happy to visit with her. After he departed his office, Deborah peered up at the mezzanine level and saw Jake meeting with the Chief. The Chief handed Jake the item he had in his left hand. They appeared to have a brief conversation and the chief returned to the elevator, heading back his office. Deborah was still perched at his office when he returned. He asked her how he could be of assistance. Deborah asked if she could view the video from the executive parking garage elevator from the previous day. His response blew her away. He told Deborah that, for some inexplicable reason, the security elevator video camera feed had shorted out and was inoperable for most of the previous day. She asked him what time of the day the system went down. He responded it appears to have been offline for the entire day. He indicated the breakdown was discovered during normal routine maintenance checks that were performed once each day prior to the opening of the building at 6 AM. Deborah couldn't believe what

70

she was hearing; and of course, the thought of Jake meeting with the security officer and them exchanging something immediately conjured up thoughts of a true conspiracy.

Deborah's frustration level was starting to boil over as she made her way to the front elevator on the way to her office on the sixth floor. As she walked to the elevator, she felt the vibration of her cell phone located in the top outer pocket of her topcoat. She pulled it out and hit accept and her good friend JoAnn yelled into the phone "Deborah, where are you?" The reception was lost once Deborah stepped onto the elevator. For six floors Deborah was wondering why JoAnn was in such a frantic state. As soon as Deborah stepped off the elevator she hit redial and got the shock of her life. Deborah had just stepped into her office when JoAnn came back on the line. JoAnn's voice was now three octaves higher than before when she asked, "did you jam your stiletto into his crotch….?" Deborah realized somehow, she had accidentally pocket dialed JoAnn yesterday afternoon while in the elevator with Jake. Now her voice tone was just as energized as JoAnn's because she realized she had the evidence she needed to take Jake down. Apparently, Joann had listened in on the entire episode in the elevator. Better yet, JoAnn clicked on her utility recorder feature to capture the entire recording. JoAnn indicated she immediately tried to call Deborah back, but all her calls went directly to voicemail.

Apparently, Deborah's phone had run out of juice and fortunate for her the charge was sufficient enough to record the entire sordid event in the elevator. Deborah lavished multiple "Thank Yous" on JoAnn for her support and asked that she maintain the utmost confidentiality. And of course, she asked that she place the recording on a thumb drive for safe keeping. JoAnn agreed and asked if there was anything else she could do. Deborah assured her she was a true friend and life saver. She promised her when things settled down, she would send her an airline ticket to fly from San Antonio to New York and their shopping trip would be on her. After hanging up Deborah broke into her happy dance.

Chapter 13

Homeward Bound

While Deborah waited for her Uber driver, her mind drifted. She wondered about the emotional toll her elevator experience might have on her Mom. She hoped to use the hour-plus ride to Stanford to rehearse; for the hundredth time, how she planned to share that· elevator experience. The fact she would have to relive the entire experience herself had led her to put off her visit home for as long as she had. She made it a practice to visit her Mom at least once a month since her Dad's passing over two years ago. Deborah had decided not to discuss the incident with her Mom until they were together face to face, but now after two months since the incident, she had finally built up her courage. Her mom had only been retired 6 months prior to her Dad's passing. Both her Mom and Dad were looking forward to their retirement years after spending 30 years building their and navigating their successful civil rights law practice in Stanford. Deborah knew her Mom had started to experience early stages of dementia.

It had become apparent to Deborah that the deterioration of her Mom's short-term memory had begun to take its toll. On her last visit home over two months ago her Mom had asked her to call their law office to see what time they could expect her Dad to arrive for dinner. Deborah's Dad had passed over a year prior. Deborah hoped what she was about to share with her Mom would conveniently fade. Deborah was able to see the arrival of the Uber driver from her living room window. As she approached her Uber vehicle, the driver activated the gulf wing rear doors of his silver Tesla and escorted Deborah with her duffel bag into the back seat. Off they headed north across the GW.

At 6 PM, (some hour and half later) Deborah arrived at the family estate. Her Mom saw and heard the Uber vehicle pull onto the circular gravel covered driveway and she immediately came to the front door to meet her. Her Mom had a smile on her face that could light up the soon to be dark early evening. She gave Deborah a big hug and gave her only daughter a kiss on the cheek. The hug seem to last for a minute or two; and finally Deborah said, "I need to let this driver get on his way", as she reached into her purse, pulled out a $20 bill, gave it to the driver and thanked him as he prepared to get back in the vehicle to lower the gulf wing rear doors. As the Tesla made it's way out of the driveway Deborah and her Mom made their way into the house.

Deborah's Mom, now 82 years old, still lived alone; but it was obvious to Deborah as she proceeded through the foyer the usually impeccable house was now somewhat cluttered and neglected. She knew her Mom would be better off having someone reside with her or at least have someone come to the house on a regular basis to help her maintain the 6000 square foot house. Deborah placed her duffle bag in the foyer as Mom said, "How about some dinner?" Her Mom knew how much of a fan Deborah was of Pepe's Pizza. Her Mom indicated she had her favorite Pepe's veggie delivered only minutes ago. Deborah made her way over to the wine pantry to the left of the dining room and pulled from the shelf a bottle of her favorite Argentine Malbec. Individually they both devoured two slices of pizza and between the two of them they consumed the entire 750ML bottle of wine. They made their way over to the great room where Deborah tuned the Sonos system to play her Mom's smooth Jazz playlist. Deborah decided to retrieve another bottle of Malbec from the wine pantry to help booster her courage as she prepared to share her elevator horror experience.

As they settled on opposite ends of the couch Deborah indicated she wanted to share something with her, but she wanted her to know she was preparing to take the appropriate steps to deal with the issue. Deborah knew in her heart those appropriate steps had yet to manifest itself. She went on to share the sordid details of her encounter with her boss, Jake. Deborah could feel her Mom's hurt as tears began to flow down her cheeks. Deborah slid over on the coach next to her Mom and they both began to sob. Her Mom knew she, and her deceased husband had fought over 30 years for the civil rights of those who were maligned and discriminated in the public domain. Now she was hearing from her own daughter that she had experienced such a horrific assault. They hugged one another for minutes until Deborah excused herself to retrieve her cell phone from her duffel bag. As Deborah returned with her phone in hand, she indicated to her Mom she wanted to share with her a photo of a young man she had met that was attempting to do business with MLB. What came next was startling to Deborah. Her Mom asked her in a somewhat cheerful tone, "Well how are things going in the world of Major League Baseball?" Deborah realized what she had just shared with her Mom had completely vanished from her memory. In one sense Deborah was relieved but deep inside she still wanted her Mom to empathize with her, if not but for a few more minutes.

Deborah shared the digital copy of the photo that was sent to her when the young man showed up originally at MLB headquarters to meet with her. Her Mom was quick to point out how handsome the young man was, and she asked was he married and what type of work did he do. But just in the midst of her fury of questions, she took a drawn out pause and said to Deborah, "This young man looks eerily familiar to a young man I met some 40 plus years ago when I was in law school. Deborah asked her Mom, "Was he someone special?" Her Mom indicated he was an undergraduate student at Brown at the time when he showed up at your Great Great Grandpa, Moncalm's house in Providence to talk to him about a baseball player that played one game for the Major League team that use to play in Providence. Her Mom went on to say Grandpa Moncalm was well into his 90's at the time and in the latter stages of Alzheimer's but strangely enough when this young man mentioned the ballplayers name Grandpa Moncalm miraculously began to describe in great detail a series of events that took place some 80 years prior in the late 1870's. Deborah was stunned that her Mom herself could recall an incident from over 40 years ago in such detail. She decided to test her Moms long-term memory acuity by asking her what sort of events did Grandpa Moncalm share with the student.

Deborah didn't have to pursue her line of inquiry because her Mom went on to share with her in great detail the fact this baseball player at Brown was signed to a one day contract to play for the Providence Grays of the National League in the summer of 1879. Grandpa Moncalm at 12 years old was the clubhouse boy. Grandpa shared with the Brown student how well the ball player performed in the game and what may have happened to him following the game. Deborah interjected, "What happened?" Her Mom went on to say the ballplayer turned up missing and was never heard from again. Grandpa went on to point out the ballplayer had given him the cap he wore during the game and how the teams manager had given him the tobacco stained jersey he wore during the game and the games lineup card for that night's games. Her Mom went on to say how despondent Grandpa was when the student left his house because he had a suspicion the red neck players who had played with the ballplayer were out to do harm to the player, but that he was afraid to share his thoughts with the authorities. Deborah was amazed at the level of detail her Mom was able to recount of her encounter with a Brown student some 40 years ago.

Deborah ended the conversation with her Mom as she took the last sip of her Malbec and started to make her way to her upstairs bedroom, pausing to thank her Mom for her continued love and understanding knowing well her Mom had in all likelihood had already forgotten her ordeal at MLB headquarters.

Chapter 14
Road Trip

Thursday, March 24, 2018, Deborah opened her email to find Lynn's message advising her, per Jake's direction, she had setup an overnight meeting for dinner next Thursday, in Philadelphia to host Phillies majority owner, Bill McMonicgle. The venue was set for the Brasserie Parc Bistro at the foot of Rittenhouse Square. As one of the top restaurants in Philadelphia, the Parc had earned a renowned reputation for its exquisite culinary dining experience. It was not uncommon there to rub shoulders with the who's who in the City of Brotherly Love. Lynn's email went on to indicate she would follow-up with Deborah once she finalized the hotel accommodations. She also indicated she would be securing the Azalea Metro North Amtrak roundtrip tickets for her and Jake. Deborah sent a reply email to Lynn confirming the receipt of her email while also complimenting her on the selection of the Parc as the restaurant venue. Having spent the first four years of her career in Philadelphia she was quite familiar with the Rittenhouse Square restaurant district.

Deborah hoped to combine a little pleasure with business while on her stay in Philly. She decided to reach out to her good friend and law school classmate, Linda Verdun, who decided to return to her Philadelphia roots to launch her law career with the prestigious law firm of Wilmont and Graham after completing law school at Brown University over ten years ago. Deborah decided to text Linda to see if she would be available next Thursday. She received an immediate response from Linda saying she was available next Thursday. She also invited Deborah to stay at her condo and encouraged her to plan for a spa day on Friday. Her response brought a smile to Deborah's face. Deborah hit the reply tab on her I-watch typing "you are on."

Later in the day, Deborah received a second email from Lynn confirming the details of the Philly road trip. The communication detailed the Amtrak train and dinner arrangements for the Philadelphia road trip. Departure from Penn station at 2 PM and dinner was confirmed for the Parc at 6 PM for their dinner meeting with Bill McMonicgle, President of the Philadelphia Phillies. Lynn also informed Deborah that hotel arrangements were set for her and Jake at Riddenhouse Square Inn. Deborah immediately texted Lynn to advise her that she had already made her own lodging accommodations for her stay in Philadelphia next week. Deborah also advised Lynn she would reach out to the Ridden House Inn to cancel her reservation. Deborah immediately called the hotel and the reservationist retrieved the reservation and advised Deborah she would cancel one of the adjoining rooms. Deborah was a bit miffed to find out an adjoining room arrangement had been set-up by Lynn. She knew this set-up had to have been orchestrated by Jake. She thought to herself what a relief it was to be able to spend time with Linda and not have to put up with Jake's bull-shit. Just the thought of being in the same space with Jake was repulsive to her on every level. Her mental acuity flip-flopped as she reflected on the thought of hanging out with her good friend Linda. Spending quality time with Linda would definitely be the high point of her road trip to Philadelphia.

On Thursday, March 31st, Deborah boarded the Azalea Metro North south bound at the Greenwich station heading to Philadelphia. The train pulled into Grand Central at 10:45 AM. Deborah received a text from Jake prior to her arrival at Grand Central directing her to take the subway from Grand Central to Penn Station and once she arrived she needed to head over to track 15 where their Amtrak Philadelphia bound train would be departing.

She was directed to join him in the dining car at the front of the train. Deborah reached the dining car at 11:55 AM. Jake greeted Deborah and asked her to join him for lunch. Deborah indicated she had a late breakfast and only wanted to have a cup of coffee. As Jake devoured his BLT, he pointed out to Deborah their visit with Bill McMonicgle was to hopefully garner his support of the training site proposal that was presented to the Executive Competition Committee two weeks prior. Deborah asked Jake if this meeting was to be the litmus test for whether or not he, Jake, was on board with the idea. Jake said he liked the idea but having Bill McMonicgle on board was critical in gaining the buy-in of the other owners. Deborah knew Jake didn't have the gravitas with the owners as a whole to pull this off but having someone like Bill McMonicgle who was viewed as the Jerry Jones of MLB owners would go a long way in convincing all the other owners to agree to the proposal.

After consuming his lunch, Jake began a nonstop round robin of calls and texts that kept him busy until they arrived at Philadelphia's Union station. Once at Union Station, they hailed a taxi for the short 15-minute ride to the hotel. Upon arriving at the Riddenhouse Square Inn, the bellman asked if they were checking in and whether or not they required any assistance with their bags. Jake immediately responded, "yes." When Deborah stated she wanted her bags to remain at the bell stand, Jake appeared to be jolted out of his jovial mood. Apparently, Lynn had neglected to share with him Deborah's text noting she had made other lodging arrangements. Jake asked her what had changed. She told him she advised Lynn she would be staying with a law school classmate who lives and practices in Philadelphia. As Jake made his way into the hotel, Deborah informed him she would be making some return calls from the lobby and would rendezvous with him at 5:45 at the bell stand. Jake told Deborah she was welcomed to make her calls from his suite. Deborah respectfully declined, thinking to herself "this guy has no clue." Deborah headed inside the hotel and settled in the lounge area where she proceeded to give Linda a call.

At 5:45 PM the bellman tooted his whistle and instantly Deborah and Jake's taxi arrived curbside. Ten minutes later they arrived early at the Parc restaurant for their 6 PM dinner meeting with Phillies owner, Bill McMonicgle. Once inside the restaurant Jake and Deborah settled in at the bar. Two seats to Deborah's immediate right sat two young ladies who appeared to be in a celebratory mood. When Jake heard one of the highly inebriated ladies blurt out "F_ _k" Hillary, Jake immediately took note and said to Deborah "that's my kind of girl." Jake took it upon himself to move to the open seat to Deborah's right and to Deborah's amazement he began to engage both of them in conversation. Deborah was utterly shocked at what she heard Jake say next, "Ladies would you care to join us for dinner?" Still stunned by his audacity, Deborah looked to her left and sees Bill McMonicgle walk into the restaurant.

Deborah and Jake moved from the bar and Jake's newfound friends to greet Bill. After their usual customary social greetings, they were shown to their table with the two intoxicated ladies in tow. Needless to say, Bill's facial expression said it all. He graciously introduced himself to the smashed young ladies at the table who fortunately had no idea that he was the owner of the Philadelphia Phillies. Jake excused himself to go to the men's room located on the second floor. Bill took it upon himself to seize the moment. He immediately pulled a $100 bill from his wallet and handed it to one of the ladies and said in a fatherly voice "Ladies it looks like you've had a full day so why don't you grab a taxi and head back to your hotel." It didn't take much encouragement once they got a glimpse of the $100 in Bill's hand. In an instant they were up and out the door.

Deborah saw firsthand how quickly Bill McMonicgle could defuse a situation that potentially could have been quite embarrassing to all of them, especially for Bill in light of his celebrity status in Philadelphia. Jake rejoined them at the table and asked Bill "what happened to the ladies?" Bill said the ladies had had a long day and they wanted to get back to their hotel. Jake was a bit surprised but quickly shifted his attention to the business at hand. After two

Makers Marks and coke Jake went on to describe the training site proposal to Bill. Deborah weighed in by pointing out the group that was going to orchestrate this initiative had been fully vetted with a resume that included their participation as the chief architect of 2016 World games. Bill was quick to state he fully supported the idea of his players, who remained unsigned, having the opportunity to attend a training venue authorized by MLB.

After an incredible French American fusion dining experience, Jake encouraged Bill to join him and Deborah at the Vault night club, one block north of the restaurant. Deborah, knowing her classmate Linda, was awaiting her call for pickup instructions and was quick to say, "Why don't you boys go on and enjoy the rest of the evening." Jake promised Bill "just one drink and we'll call it a night." Bill said "ok, one drink." Deborah said her goodbyes as she entered her taxi heading back to the hotel to meet Linda and retrieve her luggage, Bill and Jake starting walking north in the direction of the Vault night club.

At 9:45 PM, Linda pulled up to the hotel valet stand in her flaming red Audi A8 Quattro convertible. When she saw Deborah, she hopped out of the car and gave her good friend a huge sisterly hug. Deborah retrieved her luggage from the bell stand, tossed it in Linda's ride and off they went. It was obvious they had a lot of catching up to do. As they headed down the Schuylkill Parkway it didn't take Linda long to realize her good friend's anxiety level was off the chain. Linda remarked "Ok, let it out." Deborah responded, "You are not going to believe the stunt my boss, Jake, pulled at dinner tonight." She went on to share the sordid details of the two funky drunk diners Jake invited to join them for dinner. Linda couldn't believe what she was hearing. She implored to Deborah to get as far away from this guy as soon as she could. Deborah promised when the time and situation was right, she would definitely make that move.

Once back at Linda's condo they popped open a bottle of Napa's finest non-oak, Kopriva Chardonnay. Linda had always been a connoisseur of fine wines and this one was no exception. After consuming three bottles of Kopriva, Deborah asked Linda for her sisterly and legal opinion on something that she hadn't shared with anyone except her good friends JoAnn and Bill. Linda quickly picked up on the Bill piece. Deborah shared with Linda who Bill was and how their relationship has begun to blossom. Linda said it's about time she found that someone special. She was so happy for her college roommate. Linda sensed there was something else Deborah was eager to share with her. Before she breeched the subject Deborah painfully began to chronicle the episode she experienced on the elevator when Jake exposed himself and verbally assaulted her. Linda's immediate reaction, "That asshole", summed up where her head was. She was obviously extremely disheartened that her good friend had gone through such a heinous experience. Linda's disgust seemed to rekindle the pain and humiliation that Deborah felt as she endured her encounter with Jake in the elevator. Linda reiterated the previous advice she gave Deborah while in the car when she shared her earlier dinner experience at the Parc restaurant. "Get as far away from this guy as you can as soon as you can." Deborah's eyes welled up with tears as she thanked Linda for her ongoing support and friendship.

Once Deborah was able to gather herself, she sheepishly shared with Linda "There is someone." Linda, still soaking in Deborah's comment, put down her glass of wine and placed both hands over her month while screeching an audible,"Girrrrl!", which drew an approving smile to Deborah's face. Linda's voice tone now two octaves higher said, "Who is he?" Deborah said, "It's a long story." Linda said, "Hold up. Let me top off my glass. We've got all night so take your time." Deborah began to share with Linda her initial encounter with Bill at the MLB Headquarters. "I was asked to be a part of a last minute executive competition meeting to evaluate a marketing proposal from Bill Williams Sports agency. I didn't think too much about my involvement in the meeting, thinking perhaps the thought was there may be a legal matter that may need to be addressed. But just prior to the start of the meeting, I got this text from the lobby security station indicating there was a Mr. Bill Williams waiting in the lobby. As I scrolled down the message on my iPhone, I come across a photo of this 'fine' brother. I have to tell you, my initial reaction to the text was why was I being assigned as "Miss Girl Friday" to escort Mr. Williams from the lobby to the 6th floor conference; but once I viewed the brother's photo, I was more than willing to accept the assignment. I quickly grabbed my nametag and strategically positioned it on my suit jacket where my Chief Legal Counsel title could be seen. From the very first time I laid my eyes on him at the lobby elevator, I was saying to myself 'it would be awfully nice to get to know him better'." Linda was quick to point out, "I've never known you to be so infatuated with someone you've only known for such a short time. He must be something." "So far, he's been so supportive in helping me through this situation with Jake", Deborah responded. Linda asked, "How did he take the news on what happened in the elevator?" Deborah thought for a moment and said, "He was furious. I got the feeling he was ready to head over to Jakes's office and beat the hell out of him. I'd have to say I would have paid to see Jake get his butt whipped." Linda said, "I'm so happy for you; it sounds like Bill's a good catch. Deborah said, "Yeah. I think so too." Deborah told Linda their spa day would start off with a total hair, nails and massage treatment at Philadelphia's premiere spa, Panache Hair and Beauty Salon located at Rittenhouse Square. Deborah had orchestrated each detail earlier in the week with her good friend and proprietor, Frank Allen, who assured her that his best staff members would be at their service.

The ladies were out and about early the next morning starting with a light breakfast at DK diner prior to arriving at Panache for their pampering session. Deborah's cell phone was set on vibrate when she noticed Jake's number stream across. There was no way she was going to allow Jake to spew his negativity today of all days. As she and Linda prepared to pamper themselves, she noticed a text message from Jake that put a smile on her face… "Have a great Day… moving forward with training site proposal." Deborah said to Linda "It's going to be an even better day." Her first thought was "Mission accomplished." She shared with Linda that the proposal they reviewed with the owner of the Phillies would be moving onto the executive board for approval. Deborah decided she would wait to give Bill Williams the good news once the executive committee had rubber stamped the approval of his training site proposal.

Chapter 15

Dreams are Forever

Two days later having returned to her flat in Harlem, Deborah was tossing and turning and couldn't seem to escape the bizarre nightmare she found herself in. The dream had her sitting with Great Grandpa Moncalm in his living room just as this young college student was leaving his house. Grandpa was uncharacteristically in high spirits after his conversation with the Brown University student who had come to the house to inquire about the college ballplayer that had played in his first Major League game for the Providence Grays of the National League.

As the front door shut behind the departing student Grandpa all of a sudden blurted out "I wanted that ballplayer to know that game jersey I issued him was clean even though the remnants of tobacco stains that were splattered on the front of the jersey in the middle of the "G" had remained even after several washings of the jersey." Suddenly Deborah broke out of her nightmare in a cold sweat and something immediately came to mind. She reflected on the vintage jersey encased in the plexi-glass case, located in Jake's current office. It just happened to have the letter "G" on the front right side of the jersey. She immediately logged on to her lap top at her bedside and googled Providence Major League Baseball team and wouldn't you know the jersey in the commissioner's office was an exact replica of the jersey worn by the 1879 Providence Grays National League baseball team. Her thoughts started racing as she contemplated whether or not the vintage jersey in the conference room could actually be one of the game worn jerseys of the 1879 Grays, and what if it was the actual jersey of the missing ballplayer, Bill White. She marveled at the thought that it could be possible. She thought to herself, "What would be the odds that this jersey was authentic and how in the world did this particular jersey come into Jake's possession?"

It dawned on Deborah, the Jersey in question was scheduled to be repositioned to the newly appointed commissioner's conference room just outside of Jake's new digs. The next thought was a lightning bolt. She hastily got going and made her way into the office. Her first stop was to head directly to Lynn's office where she greeted Lynn with the usual office pleasantries. Deborah asked her how the transition was going. Lynn indicated all was going well. As she was talking with Lynn she peered over Lynn's shoulder and saw that the Jersey was still hanging in Jake's old office. She asked Lynn if Jake planned to move the jersey, all the while knowing that he definitely planned on moving his prized piece to its new home located in the commissioner's conference room. Deborah was quick to share with Lynn that when she had her office redecorated last year, she had an excellent experience using a local Two Guys and a Truck Moving Company. Deborah offered to reach out to her mover on Lynn's behalf. Lynn was so appreciative and relieved that Deborah's offer to help would give her one less thing on her plate to handle.

Deborah headed back to her office and called her guy Sherm at Two Guys. Sherm was ecstatic to hear from his former client, Ms. Deborah, not just for the prospect of gaining additional business but now in his late 70's, he could only fantasize about being in the same space with such a drop-dead gorgeous woman as Deborah. Sherm didn't know it, but Deborah was counting on his attraction to her to enable her to get her hands on the Jersey. Deborah gave Sherm Lynn's contact information and encouraged him if he got the job to be certain to stop by and say hello while he was in the building. Sherm didn't have to be asked twice.

One week later, Deborah gets a knock on her door and low and behold it was Sherm. She invited him to have a seat in her office. Sherm thanked her for the referral and indicated that his crew would be conducting the move this upcoming weekend. Deborah indicated she was glad things worked out. She asked Sherm if Lynn would be meeting them on Saturday. He replied they were to meet with security downstairs, and they would be escorted up to the sixth floor. Deborah thought to herself Saturday would have to be the day she would make her move. And that move would require the assistance of her longtime childhood friend, NYPD Director of Forensic Services, Dr. Ramona Green.

Deborah knew timing was going to be tight, but doable. She knew it was now or never. She thought first things first and placed a call to her good friend Ramona's mobile phone. When Ramona answered, Deborah said "long time no talk." Ramona responded that it was always good hearing from her. Deborah asked Ramona how were things going over at NYPD? Ramona said she had just gotten off a call with her good friend Max at the canine center. Unfortunately, Max was agonizing over the fact he was being forced to retire several of his existing K9 dogs, many of which had contributed several years of service to the agency. The canine team was currently in the process of training a number of new dogs that would eventually replace his entire K9 squad. Ramona indicated she tried to humor him by saying his current K9 squad had earned their well-deserved retirement. But Max didn't warm up to the banter, he knew it would take a while before the new dogs would be up to speed.

Ramona asked, "So what's up with you?" Deborah cleared her throat and went on to share with Ramona all that had occurred in the elevator. As Deborah was sharing all the sordid details Ramona's stomach started to do flip flops. Ramona and Deborah had grown up together and were like sisters. Ramona asked Deborah if there was anything she could do to help her. Deborah said well, matter of fact, there was something she needed that required her professional expertise. Ramona asked how could she help? Deborah shared with

Ramona she had an item of clothing that she needed to have analyzed for potential DNA specimens. Ramona was a little surprised by the request. She knew Deborah was a very thoughtful and analytical person who was not known to be prone to jump to foregone conclusions. Ramona paused for a second and said, "You aren't kidding", Deborah said, "I couldn't be more serious." Ramona asked where the item was and how much time she would have the item at her disposal to complete the DNA analysis. Deborah shared with Ramona, "This is where things get a little tricky." Ramona paused and asked, "How so?" Deborah informed Ramona the item to be tested was located in the new Commissioner's office. Ramona was shocked that her good friend was about to cross a line of no return. Deborah indicated she would have less than an hour to complete the analysis and, by the way, the item could not leave the premises.

Ramona skeptically said "Girlfriend you have just left the reservation. Even if it were possible the risk for potential damage to the item is a real possibility. Are you truly willing to take the risk?" Deborah said she was more determined than ever. Ramona could tell in Deborah's voice there was no turning back. "So, what's the plan?" It was her intent to have Ramona position her mobile equipment in her office early Saturday morning. At around noon Deborah indicated she would invite the moving crew on the 6th to join her for a free catered lunch on the 3rd floor at the opposite end of the building. That would be the opening to remove the Plexiglas case which contains the jersey that is to be culled for DNA specimens. Ramona shook her head and said "Only for you would I even attempt such a feat. What do you hope to discover that is so damn important that you would risk your entire career and mine as well?" Deborah's voice started to crack when she said, "As you said, it's that important to me that I would risk everything." "Wow, you are insane." Deborah asked, "Does that mean you will do it?" Ramona confided in "Deborah, we've been friends all our lives and maybe one day you'll choose to share with me why this jersey is so damn important." Deborah assured Ramona if her assumption proved to be true a long overdue debt would be finally paid.

Saturday, at 9 AM, when Ramona arrived, it was a balmy 60 degrees in Manhattan and not a cloud in the sky. It wasn't unusual that Deborah would drop by her office as she made her normal 5K power walk on the Upper East Side every Saturday morning. From her office window that overlooked Park Avenue she could see Ramona's NYPD van pull up to the curb and immediately her driver opened the van's sliding side door and rolled out what appeared to be a miniature x-ray machine. In less than 5 minutes Ramona and her mobile x-ray looking machine were at Deborah's 6th floor office door. Deborah gave Ramona a hug and handed her a café Latte from Starbucks. Deborah said, "how about a tour?"

Generally, on Saturdays, the office is a ghost town but today was even more so because the entire executive staff was in Arizona attending the owners' meeting. Deborah and Ramona with Latte in hand headed over to the conference room and down to Jake's office where the jersey was still hanging, but by this afternoon would be moved to its new location in the new commissioner's conference room just across the foyer on the 6th floor. Ramona pointed to the Jersey saying, "So this is it." Deborah shared with Ramona that she thought the jersey was a vintage jersey that could have been worn by a former Major League Player. Deborah indicated as far as she knew it was an 1879 Providence Gray team jersey. "So, what's the deal?" Deborah told Ramona once she did her thing hopefully, they both would have an answer to that question. They headed back to her office. Deborah peered out the window and there was the Two Guys crew curbside unloading their gear. It was now about 10 AM. By the time Sherm's crew made their appearance at Jake's office it was almost 10:15 AM. Deborah made her way over to Jake's office to say hello. Needless to say Sherm was pleasantly surprised to see Ms. Deborah. Deborah put on the charm and invited Sherm and his three-man crew to a catered lunch in the third-floor cafeteria. Sherm graciously accepted the invitation which they agreed would be at 12:30 PM.

The stage was set. At 12:25 PM Deborah made her way across the foyer to rendezvous with Sherm's crew to escort them downstairs to the 3rd floor. As the elevator on the 6th floor closed with Deborah and the crew headed down, Ramona rolled her machine across the foyer into Jake's office. At this time, the Plexiglas case was on the floor leaning on the back wall. Ramona immediately pulled out her battery-operated drill and unbolted the case. She went on to surgically remove the jersey and gingerly positioned it on top of the forensic scanner where she proceeded to scan the front and then the rear of the jersey. In less than 30 seconds per side she repositioned the jersey back in its case. She quickly rounded up her equipment and proceeded down the hall, onto the elevator and down to the first floor where her driver waited curbside. Through the sliding door went the equipment, Ramona hopped into the front passenger seat and off they went. Ramona had accomplished her task in less than 30 minutes.

Deborah and the moving crew made their way back upstairs at approximately 1:15 PM at which time Deborah said her goodbyes' knowing Ramona had successfully left the building. Sherm graciously thanked Deborah for her hospitality, and he and his crew headed back to complete the moving job.

Chapter 16

DNA for Two

On September 19, 2018 at 9:00 AM the entire MLB competition committee gathered in the executive conference room adjacent to the new commissioner's office in anticipation of Bill Williams' presentation. Bill was no stranger to this group who just six months earlier he presented his groundbreaking, barnstorming proposal, to no avail. Thanks to Deborah he would find out later his proposal was dead on arrival. But today was a new day, and a totally new proposal was on the table. In actuality, to Bill's way of thinking, this new proposal would accomplish his ultimate objective at a much lower cost structure and liability exposure to his team. As before, the challenge was to convince the committee this new proposal was in the best interests of MLB and their owners. But this time things were different.

Deborah had provided key intel that gave Bill confidence this new proposal had better odds of being given serious consideration by the committee. As Bill prepared to present his power point presentation to the group, he couldn't help but notice the tobacco stained baseball jersey encased in the plexi-glass cube just to the right of the presentation screen. He remembered from his earlier visit that it was previously located in the Vice Commissioner's office across the hall. His thoughts drifted for just a moment to whether this jersey was the real deal or a vintage replica. His slight indulgence was interrupted when the newly appointed Commissioner, Jake Everhardt, entered the conference room.

The day prior to the meeting Deborah received a text from her good friend Ramona at NYPD forensic advising her she had recovered three DNA samples, two human and one plant life from the Providence Grays Jersey. She went on to say that now the challenge becomes matching the DNA specimens. At this point she and Ramona had been playing phone tag and had yet to speak to each other to discuss Ramona's findings. Needless to say, Deborah's internal neurons were in overdrive. After receiving Ramona's text her motivation for attending this meeting had taken on a whole new dimension. Of course, as part of the Competition Committee she served in an official capacity; and she was expected to be in attendance. Now, however, after receiving her much anticipated text from Ramona, she decided to act on a premonition she remembered from her dream. She strategically positioned herself at the conference table directly across from where she expected Jake to be seated. Her focus was to intently observe Jake's every movement with the hope of capturing a specimen of Jake's DNA by retrieving his coffee cup or napkin. She realized her unscientific rudimentary forensic protocol may prove to be fruitless but that was the only opportunity she felt would come her way anytime soon… so she decided to go for it.

Jake settled in at the head of the conference table where Deborah anticipated he would be seated. He began the meeting by welcoming everyone and reintroducing Bill Williams to the committee members who were present when Bill pitched his Barnstorming tour proposal. Bill clicked on his first slide which introduced his Dream Team along with a scaled down bio for each team member. Bill wanted the committee to know up front that each member of his team was extremely accomplished in their various fields of endeavor. Next, he asked Lynn, Jakes' administrative assistant, to assist him by passing out to each committee member a spiral bound booklet which captured the entire power point slide presentation. Bill moved swiftly through his presentation, although in great detail. He described how his team proposed to put in place multiple training sites akin to most major league sites in Arizona and Florida. Each proposed site would allow up to 120 active roster players including free agents who remained unsigned to have a place to train as they prepared for the upcoming season when the strike eventually came to an end. Bill was quick to point out the expense to bring these camps on board would be borne by advertisers. When Bill concluded his presentation, he felt a totally different vibe in the room than when he presented to the group before. There was complete silence until Jake voiced his concern regarding the branding of these camps. He would want MLB to be recognized as the ambassador of this initiative and MLB would in all likelihood expect to receive some additional remuneration on the backend from Bill's organization.

As Jake was talking Bill was thinking to himself this guy is all about image and screwing the little guy. Jake concluded by saying to his committee members in attendance, "It's obvious Bill and his team have given this committee a creative approach to deal with the current labor impasse between the owners and players' union situation. He went on to say, "I would recommend the committee consider moving this proposal on to the executive committee for further discussion." It was music to Bill's ears. Jake turned to Bill and thanked him for his time and indicated he could expect to hear from MLB Executive Committee within a week.

Jake announced, "Meeting adjourned." At that point Jake took one final sip from his coffee and proceeded to leave the room. Deborah maintained a keen eye on Jake's coffee cup that remained at the head of the table. As Bill prepared to depart, he completed repacking his handheld Pond Projector and Wave unit which enabled Bill's team to join in on the presentation from remote locations around the world. Their ability to add data and footnotes live as the presentation was taking place, really got the attention of the MLB executives in attendance.

As the meeting room emptied out Bill felt comfortable enough to ask Deborah, "How do you think it went?" Deborah signaled thumbs up. This brought a smile to his face that could have lit up the entire room. Bill was just about to leave the room when he realized he had one sip of coffee left in his cup. He sipped the last drop of his coffee and placed the cup back down on the table. Unbeknownst to Deborah he placed his cup nearest to where Jake had already sat his cup. Bill said his goodbye and left the room. Quickly Deborah made her move to remove Jake's cup and place it in a padded bag she pulled from her briefcase under the table. Once at the head of the conference table she noticed two coffee cups, side by side. She hadn't planned for this, so she quickly decided to gingerly place both cups in the padded bag just as the catering staff entered the room.

Chapter 17

Ask, Seek, Knock

Matthew 7:7 NIV

"Ask and it will be given to you

Seek and you will find

Knock and the door will be opened to You"

Bill went Asking, Seeking and Knocking ... He knew time was of the essence to bring his dream team on board to pull together his Spring Training proposal. Fortunately, his first thought was to blast text four of his closest friends and past business Associates: Deshaun Anthony, Gayle Wells, LeRoy Jackson and Julie Shields. All these individuals had already distinguished themselves as trail blazers in their respective fields of endeavor. Bill had at one time or another either collaborated and or partnered with one or more of these individuals to accomplish several groundbreaking projects, both domestic and global.

Most recently Bill's team had partnered with this same group to successfully bring the 2016 Summer World Games to the Republic of Cuba. His consortium orchestrated logistics for all participating countries' athletes, site selections for each event, scheduling for all events including opening ceremony activities, lodging and meal preparation for all participants and attendees. Bill had publicly expressed, in the past, that he would be willing to go to battle with this dream team of professionals and felt confident they would be triumph.

Once back in the office Bill had Bert coordinate a Wave video chat room enabling all the stakeholders to actively interact with the PowerPoint slides Bill was about to project on the screen in his conference room. This technology also enabled each participant to see any notes or slides any of them wanted to simultaneously share with the group. Bill made everyone aware that he had previously presented a barnstorming proposal to the MLB Competition Committee that was summarily turned down. However, now he felt confident that as a team they could successfully pull together his proposed spring training initiative which in his estimation would far exceed the tangible results he had hoped to accomplish with his original barnstorming tour initiative. His first slide gave a thorough overview of the entire proposal including the aggressive timeline they would be required to meet. After Bill concluded his presentation the group unanimously agreed with Bill's assessment and timeline. In fact, as a group they felt the addition of Cuba to the training site rotations of Miami, Phoenix and Punta Cana Dominican Republic was a brilliant idea.

Bill felt this would be the opportune time to share with the group his ultimate vision and how each of them would be instrumental to the success of the project. Bill knew merging their respective talents would bring the synergy necessary to accomplish his lifelong vision. He could tell by viewing their images on his Wave screen they were anxious to hear what he had in mind. With a slight pause to add a bit more suspense to the moment, he announced to the group it was his vision to formulate and launch a competing MLB league with a Caribbean footprint in the Republic of Cuba. Bill waited for their response, but he could tell immediately the excitement and wonderment on their faces. Individually and as a group they all agreed to be a part of this historic undertaking. Bill was quick to reiterate to the group the success of their Spring Training initiative would provide the impetus and launch pad for the formulation of the new league. The Spring Training proposal would give them carte blanche access to topflight on-field and management talent in the Major Leagues. Bill reiterated to them, that pulling off the Spring Training initiative would be paramount to the survival of his proposed new league. His new dream team unanimously agreed to reach out to their respective contacts to garner key intel to support the development of the Spring Training proposal. As a group they agreed to reconnect in two days to provide initial updates.

Chapter 18

Games On

August 3, 2020

Monday 8:15 AM, the entire 6th Floor of 245 Park Avenue was bustling with media reporters and camera crews who joined the MLB executive team awaiting the start of the press briefing to announce the launch of MLB's new training sites that were scheduled to be launched in four prominent locations including Miami and Phoenix domestically and international sites in Punta Cana Dominican Republic and Havana Cuba. As Jake stepped up to the podium, he asked if everyone would grab a seat so they could begin. He went on to share with those in attendance and those streaming online that his team had been working closely with the owners and player agents to develop these unique training sites that will allow players to select the sites they choose to attend. Deborah wasn't surprised to hear that Jake was taking full credit for the training site proposal that Bill's team had brought to MLB. When Bill and his team, who were streaming the telecast, heard Jake's claim they were obviously disappointed that Jake would have the audacity to take credit for something that was a turnkey operation ready to launch. It was an insult to Bill's team, who had worked diligently to pull together the training site proposal in record breaking time, that the Commissioner would blatantly misrepresent his role as the brain trust behind the training site proposal. Bill's team, for the first time, was seeing in full view Jake's true narcissistic behavior. However, on the other hand they were ecstatic that their proposal was about to be launched with the full endorsement of MLB.

Bill's team was proud of the fact that they were able to provide the opportunity for players who, regardless of their team affiliation, would be able to participate in professionally choreographed training and conditioning to prepare them for if and when the new the season would get underway. These camps would be open to all 40-man roster players of each Major League team. The camps' duration would be a maximum of six weeks unless the labor disruption was resolved sooner. After Jake delineated the details of the program, he opened the floor for questions. The first question from the floor asked how MLB was able to keep this proposal under wraps until now and was this a precursor to the end of the labor disputes. Jake indicated the idea was only shared with a select group of owners and members of the players union. Union, knowing all along he had hijacked the idea from Bill's proposal. He went on to say that he hoped the training site proposal would help bring the owners and the players back to the bargaining table. Of course, Deborah and her fellow MLB associates were well aware Bill Williams' team had brought this turnkey opportunity to MLB for their consideration. Deborah felt sorry for Bill because she knew this was his baby. Little did Jake realize it at the time this admonition would eventually lead to his demise.

When Jake called Bill after the press conference to tell him MLB would support the training site proposal Bill acted as if he had not viewed the telecast. Bill thanked Jake for his support and reaffirmed his team commitment to flawlessly execute the plan. Jake selfishly viewed the training site proposal as his coming out party as the new Commissioner and he was not about to let anybody, or anyone tarnish his rising star.

Following the press conference Deborah also called Bill to congratulate him and his team and to offer her apologies for Jake's posturing during the briefing. Bill said, "No apology necessary." He indicated he had just gotten off the phone with Jake and was well aware of Jake's need to make everything about himself. Bill indicated he was very appreciative of the opportunity she had helped him take advantage of regardless as to who got credit. Bill knew the success of the training initiative would open the pathway for him to achieve his ultimate goal.

Estadio Latinoamericano Stadium, the Yankee Stadium of Cuba was bustling with activity. Not only were there more than 200 plus ballplayers and coaches on multiple fields, there were more than 10,000 rabid fans in the stands. Fan enthusiasm was running at an all-time high. The last time this magnitude of enthusiasm for Cuban Baseball occurred was on March 20, 2016 when both President Obama and President Fidel Castro threw out the first pitch for the Tampa Bay Rays versus the Cuban national team. Many fans appeared to be beating on some sort of drum and or blowing their brains out with those annoying plastic troubadour horns. The pageantry and nationalist spirit of the Cuban fans was at an all time high as the music and flag waving was continuous throughout the complex.

Past President and current Cuban Minister of Sports, Raul Castro, was a regular visitor to the Cuban training site. Bill knew it was in his best interest to develop a cordial relationship with Raul. It was also apparent Raul had his own thoughts on how Cuban Baseball might further enhance the transition pathway to normalization of relations between the US and Cuba. He felt baseball could be that conduit. Bill was not bashful when it came to using the influence that Raul had in Cuba to get things accomplished that could support their Cuban training site. One would say that both Bill and Raul were quite comfortable in using whatever influence they had to further their self-interest. The eventual success of the Cuban training site would provide the impetus Bill had hoped for that would set the stage to bring forward his ultimate goal of establishing a new Caribbean MLB.   He approached Raul during one of his visits to the site to share his vision to eventually establish a new Caribbean Major League with Cuba as the epicenter of the new league. Raul was ecstatic about the prospect of the new league, especially the thought of Cuba being the key player. Raul suggested as the next step that he would personally present the proposal to Cuba's new Prime Minister, Miguel Diaz-Canel. Bill was on pins and needles while he waited on word from Prime Minister Diaz-Canel regarding his proposal. Needless to say when he received word the next day that Raul had been directed to move forward he was ecstatic.

Raul shared with Bill that ever since President Obama had thrown out the first pitch during the 2016 World Games his aspirations for the furtherance of geopolitical relations with the US had been a paramount initiative for his government. He went on to say he felt his government would be in full support of this new league with the understanding Cuba would be the epicenter of the new league and would host the first championship series. Bill realized that getting Cuba on board would give him the leverage he needed to justify the buy-in from the other potential stakeholders: Puerto Rico, the Dominican Republic, Venezuela and Miami. Raul and Bill agreed to maintain the confidentiality of this initial discussion until all the stakeholders, including the player's union, had a chance to weigh-in on the proposal. They both agreed to the terms and next steps. It was not surprising all the sites under consideration for the new league footprint had performed exceedingly well during the six-week training program.

Next Steps… Bill felt like pinching himself. For better or worse, he had put his lifelong dream, to formulate a new league, in play. Now that the six-week training programs were completed, it was time to formulate his plan to bring his new league to life. In the midst of his euphoric state, Bill's cell phone began to vibrate, reflecting the number of the one person he so wanted to hear from at that moment.

Chapter 19

Five Mimosas Coming Up

Bill was just about to drift off when his Motown "My Girl" ringtone hit the first note. Yes, Deborah now had her unique ringtone that her and Bill had adopted from their own special song. He looked forward to hearing Deborah's voice and today was no exception. However, today, when he heard her voice it resonated at a much higher upbeat octave. Her first words were, "You have to feel pretty good Mr. Williams?" Bill responded, "How so?" Deborah bounced back, "Like you haven't heard that all the social media sites are abuzz with the return of baseball allbeit only in a pre-season vignette. Yes, Bill's Pre-season training exhibitions had once again renewed the interest in America's game of baseball. Bill sheepishly responded, "When you're hot you're hot." Bill had to admit the fans', players' and sponsors' reactions had far exceeded his expectation. The fact is it couldn't have gone any better." Bill was proud and pleased to hear in Deborah's voice her obvious approval and delight. Deborah's next comment was even more pleasing to his ear. Deborah asked Bill if she could treat him to lunch. To which Bill responded, "Where and when?" She said "Lure, of course." Lure had become their special rendezvous destination in the City. "How about 1PM tomorrow?" Bill was quick to respond, "You're on!" Deborah said, "Well it's a date!" The word date was sweet music to Bill's ear. Bill's blissful overnight sleep was enhanced by his anticipation of being in Deborah's presence the next day.

Needless to say, 1PM couldn't come quick enough as Bill anxiously awaited Deborah's arrival at Lure for their lunch date. Bill's lunch date with Deborah took a surprising turn when Deborah arrived at the restaurant. She was accompanied by another female who Deborah introduced as Ramona Greene, Director of NYPD Office of Forensic Services. Bill was a bit befuddled on two fronts… why had someone from the NYPD forensic department joined them for lunch and what happened to what he had envisioned as his and Deborah's romantic rendezvous. Well, at least he received a loving hug from Deborah, and he was able take in the fragrance of her signature Giorgio Armani Si as they were about to be escorted to their usual table at the rear of the dining room. The maitre' d escorted the three to the corner booth at the rear corner of the restaurant. The waiter took their drink orders, which all happened to be Mimosas.

Deborah started the conversation by reintroducing Ramona and sharing the fact that the two of them had been close friends for over twenty years. What came next caused Bill to gulp down the first of what would end up being a total of five Mimosa in rapid fire. She started out by describing her and Ramona's clandestine operation and their unbelievable discovery.

Deborah went on to drop the bomb shell that caused Bill to down his next Mimosa even quicker than the first when she said with Ramona's help and expertise they had determined with 95% accuracy that his DNA was a match with one of the human DNA specimens recovered from the Providence Grays jersey displayed in the Commissioner's office. Bill remembered seeing the jersey in a plexi-glass case when he made his first visit to the MLB headquarters. Bill said, "How could this be? But wait what's going on here? What's the interest in collecting DNA specimens from the Commissioner's jersey?"

Deborah went on to tell Bill and Ramona about the story her great grandfather, Moncalm shared with her Mom about the Brown University student who played in a Major League baseball game for the Providence Grays of the National League during the 1879 season.

He had shared with her the conversation he had with the ballplayer, Bill White, after the game just as he was about to depart the locker room. Her great grandfather asked him to autograph the cap for him that he wore during the game and the manager was kind enough to give Bill the jersey he wore and the lineup card from the game. Deborah said the one thing her great grandfather shared with her Mom regarding the description of the jersey was that it had three tobacco stains within the letter "G" on the jersey. Deborah indicated to Bill that when the College student paid her great grandfather a visit during his college days at Brown, he sparked some deep-seated memories that her great grandfather had intentionally suppressed in his sub-conscience for more than eight decades. He knew the three "redneck" ballplayers that followed Bill White, after he left the locker room, were up to no good. He suspected that they had overheard him and Bill talking about Bill's parents back in Georgia not being there to see him play and how it was too difficult for them to travel from down South for whatever reason. He knew his parents would have taken great pride to see him play. Grandpa sensed the boy was part colored, and he also knew for him to share his true identity with anyone was a major risk.

The fact that from a pure genealogist aspect there is no question that had Bill White's true heritage been known he would have unquestioningly gone down in history as the first Black and Slave to play in the Major Leagues. Grandpa had this feeling that one day his autographed cap would become a treasured possession. Deborah described Grandpa's frustration of not fully cooperating with the authorities. He felt so ashamed when the authorities came to question him regarding the apparent disappearance of Bill White. He was fearful of potential reprisals if he told them he had seen the three players follow Bill out of the locker room. The authorities asked him what Bill had with him when he left the locker room. He told them Bill took the jersey he wore the night of the game, the lineup card and his glove. The authorities advised Grandpa that the only thing they had recovered was the lineup card which they had back at the precinct.

Grandpa later heard that Bill White's parents had dispatched their own search party that arrived in the Providence area a few days after the ball player was apparently reported missing by his girlfriend. He understood the lineup card was eventually turned over to Bill's parents.

Bill was still reeling with thoughts of how he fit into this whole scheme of things. The thought of being a DNA match with someone that lived over 132 years ago was mind blowing. The sheer thought that he and his brother Bert could actually be a direct descendent of the first player of color to play baseball in a Major League Baseball game was mind blowing! Deborah asked Bill if he was aware of any mention of his ancestry dating back to the mid-eighteen hundreds. Bill told her to the best of his knowledge there was nothing he knew of that would link his family to Bill White. Bill told Deborah he would check some keepsake things his great grandmother had left his mom who had passed in 2013. He admitted he hadn't really paid close attention to the personal affects his mom had left after her passing. Bill decided in light of what he had just heard it might be a good time to check what was in the chest his mom had stored away.

Both Deborah and Ramona saw the look in Bill's eyes when the next salvo hit. Ramona indicated they had also uncovered another significant human DNA match along with a rare plant DNA specimen from the jersey as well. Bill was almost afraid to ask who the other human DNA match was. Both Deborah and Ramona said in unison said, "You are not going to believe this." Bill told them, "Try me." Ramona said the other human DNA specimen was a 95% match to Commissioner Jake. Bill's immediate thought was it would not be surprising that Jake's DNA would appear on the jersey given the Commissioner would have handled the jersey on numerous occasions while in his possession. So, what was so earth shaking about the discovery of Jake's DNA on the jersey? Ramona was quick to point out the DNA discovery was characteristic of human DNA from the mid-late 1800's time frame. Bill's attention immediately shifted on a dime when he thought to himself, "Was it plausible Jake's ancestors may have played a role in Bill White's disappearance some 132 years ago?" Bill asked Ramona if it was a stretch to think there may be some connection. Ramona pointed out that it's highly likely one of Jake's ancestors had come in contact with this particular jersey at one point in time. Ramona and Deborah continued telling Bill that the other missing piece involved the DNA of a rare plant called Rattlesnake Manna Grass that just happened to grow during the spring and fall months in the northeastern corridor of the United States. The three of them arrived at the same conclusion at the same time. The question they asked themselves was, "If this jersey had been taken from Bill White at the location where this rare plant grows, then perhaps some evidence of what really happened to Bill White could be brought to light!" The three wondered if it was worth a shot to uncover what really happened in the disappearance of Bill White.

They agreed to keep these discoveries under wraps until Bill had an opportunity to go through his family archives and Ramona took a deeper dive into the plant research regarding the actual locations and time of year the Rattlesnake Manna Grass would blossoms in the northeast corridor of the United States. Bill barely touched his lunch appetizer but did in fact knock off two more Mimosas emptying the carafe.

Chapter 20

Pops to the Rescue

After lunch with the ladies, Bill was still reeling from the sheer magnitude of Deborah and Ramona's DNA discovery. He had totally forgotten to share with Deborah the latest developments from the Latin American Countries that participated in their training site camps. The positive endorsement the new Caribbean Major League Baseball, CMLB was receiving from their Latin American partners was quite encouraging. The epicenter of the new league was to be in Cuba which fortunately had already gained the full endorsement of Cuba's Commissioners of Sports, Raul Castro and Cuba's Prime Minister, Miguel Diaz-Canel himself. Bill's initial plan for the league would be to have two teams from each of the following countries: Cuba, Puerto Rico, Dominican Republic, Venezuela and the lone US based teams would be located in Miami. The whole idea of forming a new independent league had its origins from Bill's dad, Bill Williams, Sr., who would always say to the kids he wanted to own his own baseball team that would compete in a league of their own. His aspiration hadn't stopped there; he wanted his league to compete directly with today's MLB.

Speaking of grandpa, Bill's intent was to reach out to him not only to see how he was getting along since grandma's passing some three years ago, but also to do some reconnaissance at grandpa's house in search of any family keepsakes that grandpa might have that could possibly shed some light on his ancestral link Deborah and Ramona had stumbled upon. Grandpa answered Bill's call on the first ring in his usual upbeat tone. Bill would always say "Hey grandpa, how's life treating you?" Grandpa would always say "No complaints, wouldn't do any good anyway." Bill asked him if he could swing by the house. Grandpa said, "Sure what's up?" Bill said he wanted to stop by and say hello, and he also had an interest in seeing if any of grandma's keepsakes stored away might have any insight into some of the family history. Grandpa indicated all his grandma's things were stored in the attic and he was welcomed to go through whatever he found in the attic. Bill said he could remember grandma talking about her personal chest and all her heirlooms. Grandpa said he wasn't sure about the whereabouts of the chest, but he was welcomed to come by and search what was in the attic. They agreed Bill would swing by early the next Saturday and bring him his usual Chick-Fil-A breakfast sandwich.

On Saturday at about 8: 05 AM, Bill arrived at grandpa's house in lower Harlem with sandwich in hand. Grandpa always gave Bill one of those super bear hugs that always brought back pleasant childhood memories of those fun days hanging out at the park with grandpa playing catch and shagging fly balls. Grandpa would blast balls into the outfield and his grandkids would try to emulate the likes of Willie Mays, Curt Flood and the great Roberto Clemente as they put their limited fielding skills on display. After regaining his breath, Bill asked Pop, "How are things going?", and as always Pops would say, "No complaints, and if I did no-one would give a darn." Then he would follow-up with, "You know I'm truly Blessed, I'm in the 4th quarter and still rounding the bases." Bill noticed, on the top shelf of the built-in bookshelves surrounding the 55-inch flat screen, the nine VCR tapes of the Ken Burns' Baseball Series. Bill asked Pop if he still had a VCR player. Pop said he wasn't sure but to the best of his knowledge the last time he looked at these particular tapes was well over 20 years ago.

Bill shared with Pop that his organization had successfully pulled together the MLB training site venues around the country that they hoped would lead to an eventual settlement in the 18-month ongoing labor dispute between the owners and players. Bill indicated he thought the players and owners were still far apart in their negotiations with no viable solution on the near horizon. Bill asked his grandpa, by any chance, did he know the whereabouts of any family keepsakes or mementos that great grandpa or grandma had passed down to him or grandma. Grandpa reminded Bill that the Waltham pocket watch that he passed down to him was a gift he had received from his father who had received it from his dad. He also reminded him there was an inscription inside the rear case of the watch. Bill told him that the Waltham watch had been appraised for over $8,000 and was now sitting in his Bank of America safe deposit box.

Bill hadn't thought of the Waltham watch as a possible clue but rest assured, he was determined to make his way over to his Bank America safe deposit box to check out the inscription inside the rear cover. He again thanked his Grandpa for such a beautiful timepiece. Bill asked if there was anything else. Then to Bill's surprise Grandpa told him that after grandma's passing in 2013, as he was clearing out their home prior to placing it on the market, he had recovered two metal chests that were now stored in his upstairs attic. Bill asked him what the chests contained. Grandpa indicated he never took the time to open up the chests to inspect the contents. Bill now had this intense sense of anticipation regarding what might be in the chests. Grandpa encouraged him to head up to the attic. Because the chests were quite heavy, he recommended keeping the chests upstairs to avoid having to drag them downstairs. Bill asked him if now was a good time. Grandpa said, "No better time than now."

Bill immediately headed to the 2nd floor and pulled down the retractable ladder and headed up the stairs into the attic. Bill was thankful the two attic fans had done their job to dissipate the heat. He flipped on the light and there in the right front corner of the attic sat two chests, just as Grandpa had described them. There was a folding chair leaning next to the furnace. Bill slid the chair over to the nearest chest and said a little prayer asking God to let it be his will to reveal the truth of who may have been the true patriarchs of his family.

Bill opened the lid of the first chest and began to dig his way through the numerous pieces of paper and photographs. After completing the search of the first chest, to no avail, he pulled the top chest off to the side and continued his search in the second chest. The contents in this chest appeared to be more dated. About a third of the way through the chest, Bill noticed a large brown envelope with a hand printed return address on the left top edge of the envelope--Providence Police Department on the first line and Evidence Recovery Department on the second line. To his utter amazement on the top right-hand side of the envelope was a cancelled stamp dated December 1879. At this point Bill's adrenaline was racing.

Bill could barely decipher the mailing address of the recipient because some apparent water stains had washed away some of the hand printed address. Bill was able to pick up a partial last name which appeared to say White and the city of Milner, Georgia. His hands were shaking to the point he could hardly maneuver his fingers to gingerly pull back the upper flap of the envelope to see what was inside. He pulled back the flap and pulled from inside the envelope a handwritten note from the Chief of Providence Police Department addressed to Mr. and Mrs. Bill White dated December 6, 1879. Chief Lonzy Jackson expressed his heartfelt condolences to the Whites for the apparent disappearance of their son, Bill. He went on to assure the Whites his department would continue to search for their son who had, at that point, been missing for over five months. He also indicated he was returning the enclosed Providence Grays lineup card from the game their son had competed in before he disappeared. The chief indicated it was determined their son William had this card in his possession when he was last seen leaving the Providence Gray's clubhouse. The Chief expressed his desire to pass along the lineup card to them as a cherished keepsake.

He couldn't believe what he had discovered. He took a deep breath before he began to make his way back down the ladder with the brown envelope in hand. He couldn't wait to share his discovery with Grandpa but before he shared his discovery, he swore him to secrecy until his team, which included Deborah and Ramona, were ready to go public with their findings. Bill went on to share with his Grandpa the incredible details of this link between their family and the missing baseball player. Grandpa couldn't believe what he was hearing. He sat down and began to get a bit emotional as he absorbed the magnitude of what he had just learned. It seemed to give him a great sense of pride and sorrow at the same time.

Grandpa asked Bill what was next. Bill said, "Wouldn't it be great if we could solve the mystery of the missing ballplayer." Grandpa encouraged Bill to do what he could to bring to light what actually happened to their lost family member. Bill assured his Grandpa his team wouldn't stop until they got to the truth. Grandpa said, "Son can you believe we are direct descendants of the first mixed race baseball player to ever play in a Major League baseball game?" Grandpa looked him in the eyes and said, "You've come too far to not uncover the truth of what really happened to Bill White." Pop gave Bill another one of those bear hugs, but this time he whispered in his ear, "I am so proud of you." Bill told his Grandpa he would like to keep the envelope and its contents in his possession for safekeeping. Grandpa agreed, and off Bill went, floating on cloud 9.

After leaving Pops, Bill was on such a natural high he felt as if he could have floated back to his office in midtown; but first things first, Bill needed to share the great news with Deborah and Ramona.

Chapter 21

Raul Calling

Bill couldn't wait to share with Deborah the good news regarding his reconnaissance efforts at Grandpa's house when his cell phone caller ID lit up with Phillip Braxton's text message saying, "The Big Dog is ready to eat, call me ASAP." Phillip, who generally wasn't predisposed to hyperboles, had played a key role in orchestrating the training site activities across the four sites. The crown jewel of all the training venues was the Cuban experience. Players, fans and sponsors' reactions to the Cuban training site far exceeded Bill's expectations. Bill immediately hit up Phillip on his speed dial. When Phillip answered on the first ring he appeared to be out of breath. He blurted through the phone "Raul is in …. Raul is in." Bill asked, "in for what?" Phillip responded, "He wants the new League's epicenter to be in Cuba." Over the past four years since Raul peacefully turned over the office of the Presidency to Miguel Diaz–Canel, Raul has been on an aggressive campaign to propel the prominence of Cuban Baseball onto the national stage. Phillip indicated he received a phone call from a gentleman claiming to be Raul Castro requesting a luncheon engagement for tomorrow to discuss Cuba's interest in being the epicenter of the new Caribbean Major Baseball League. Phillip encouraged Bill that they needed to strike while the iron was hot. He felt now was the time to make his way back to Cuba to meet with Raul and his commission.

Bill was well aware there were the two daily non-stop Southwest flights from JFK to Cuba that would get him comfortably to Havana early the next morning. Phillip was convinced Bill's attendance could seal the deal with the Cuban government officials. Phillip's passion for the formation of the new league was contagious. Bill indicated he would immediately make arrangements to be on the first flight out the next day. Phillip was confident he could get Bill positioned on the Commission's docket without much difficulty. Bill knew this landmark meeting had the potential to catapult his dream of launching a new league to the fore front.

Just the thought of his lifelong dream gaining traction was mind blowing. Bill was still on an emotional high now having the new found knowledge regarding his ancestral connection and coupled with the real prospect of his lifelong dream becoming a reality truly was a blessing, notwithstanding the fact that he had found the love of his life in Deborah. But in the blink of an eye Bill realized the haunting mystery of the disappearance of Edward White deserved his attention as well. He realized he couldn't deal with this alone. Then he suddenly realized that he had yet to bring Deborah and Ramona up to speed on the incredible discovery he had made at Grandpa's house. Just the thought of Deborah and Ramona's involvement to this point made him realize he would need both of them to join with him to bring to light out of darkness the true story of Edward White's disappearance.

Bill's pronouncement to Deborah while speaking to her on her cell phone was met with a resounding scream of excitement. She couldn't wait to conference in Ramona on the call but was momentarily delayed when Bill proceeded to share with her what he felt was more great news. He eagerly shared with her the call he received from Phillip regarding Raul Castro reaching out to him regarding moving forward in formulating a new Caribbean Major League Baseball organization. Deborah was stunned. She asked Bill when this idea of forming a new league came about. Bill told her he had previously discussed the idea with the Cuban International Baseball Commissioner, Raul Castro, who had become the Director of the Sports Commission in 2018 after stepping down as President.

Deborah was a bit taken aback hearing this for the first time. To put it mildly she was speechless and awestruck by the enormity of what she had just heard. Orchestrating the extended training site initiative was one thing, but establishing a competing Major League operation was unthinkable or at best a pipedream that would never fly in light of the MLB's federal anti-trust protective status within the United States. Deborah thought to herself, "Has this guy lost touch with reality. Is he that naïve to think the power brokers at MLB would ever roll over to allow the formulation of a competing league that it could see the light of day." Bill could tell by Deborah's reaction that she was a bit taken aback, and then what came next was even more astonishing to Deborah's ears as Bill smugly said, "Cuba", Deborah asked, "What do you mean Cuba? Are you saying Cuba is part of this whole notion?" Bill said, "Not only are they part, they will actually be the epicenter of the new Caribbean Major League operation. The other participants we are hoping to have in the fold are Puerto Rico, The Dominican Republic, Venezuela, Curacao and Miami. A total of twelve teams with each location providing two teams that would compete in two different divisions."

To Bill's amazement, what followed next blew him away. Deborah's mood suddenly softened when she said, "Hmmm, this might be doable... I mean this could actually work." He went on to share with her that Raul had dispatched his private plane to pick him, Bert, and Phillip up at JFK the next morning. Bill was still reflecting on Deborah's comments and decided it was the opportune time to thank her for all her support in getting him to the point where he could even think about bringing to life a competing Major Baseball League and just as important her and Ramona's efforts in discovering Edward White's jersey. For that she would have his indelible gratitude for the rest of his life. If that were not enough Bill went on to ask for her and Ramona's assistance in his search to find out what really happened to Edward White. Deborah realized Bill's desire to accomplish his lifelong dream to establish his new league combined with his passion to bring attention to the life of Edward White was a journey she felt compelled to be a part of. Her comment to Bill said it all, "Sign me up Coach", I'll be sure to reach out to Ramona to discuss possible next steps they may want to consider in their search for more details surrounding Edward White's disappearance." Bill again shared with Deborah how much he appreciated what she was doing, and without realizing it as he was about to end the call he said, "I Love you". As the dial tone went dead Deborah was still reeling from Bill's confession, that he loved her. Although this was the first time she had heard Bill verbally express his love for her she had known for some time their friendship had blossomed into something special.

The next morning at 7:05 AM as the Lear jet headed full speed down the runway, the sheer exhilaration of the lift off made the reality of the situation even more surreal for Bill, Bert and Philip. As they settled into their seats sipping their Cuban coffee lattés, and nibbling on fresh baked sopapillas, their individual thoughts were riveted on the magnitude of what they were hopeful of accomplishing during their ensuing meeting with the Cuban contingency.

Bill texted Deborah to let her know he was Cuba bound. Phillip shared with Bill and Bert their tentative itinerary for the day, and he also encouraged them to be cognizant of the political optics when it came to dealing with foreign government officials especially when dealing with a socialist government as in Cuba. Phillip knew the political optics surrounding their meeting with the Cuban contingency could have a major impact on the success of their negotiations if the proper spin control wasn't implement. Phillip also shared with them that he was more encouraged now than before because he had been contacted through back channels and told Raul Castro had taken it upon himself to reach out to the heads of state of the other potential CMBL teams to gain their conditional approval to be a part of the new league. During Raul's initial vetting of the other heads of state he strategically shared with them the three distinct revenue streams that would constitute the new league's solid financial foundation. It had been rumored since the advent of the sports betting industry that new opportunities to expand the footprint of many of the professional leagues would become available. Bill and his team were already in lock step with the key players in the Sports

Betting arena who had already come on board with substantial resources including funding and technological support in order to make the new league viable right from the beginning . Bill's team's internal forecast anticipated the potential revenue stream from sports betting would far exceed both the anticipated revenue from both corporate related sponsorships and per-paid live streaming combined.

Bill was pleasantly surprised that the new leagues' 501(c)(3) charitable foundation would greatly enhance their ability to give back to those Caribbean communities that were still in need as a result of the numerous natural disasters that had occurred in recent years. Phillip would later find out Raul had already secured a buy-in from the delegations of Puerto Rico, The Dominican Republic, Venezuela and Curacao. Bill knew having two teams located within the continental United States, preferably in the Miami area, would be the key driver for growing TV revenues in the United States. The 12-team league would compete in a 60-game wraparound season from November through February.

Wheels down. In less than two hours they had landed at the Havana Jose Marti International airport. The Lear jet taxied to a private executive gate where Bill, Bert and Phillip disembarked. To their surprise they were met by Raul Castro, himself. They exchanged greetings and loaded into Raul's limo and off they went, heading to the Royal Palace. Once at the Presidential Palace, Raul escorted them to the main conference room located on the second floor where they met with Raul's entire Cuban Sports delegation. Raul started the meeting by having his staff members introduce themselves and describe their roles and responsibility within the sports delegation. Following the introductions, Raul immediately directed the attendees attention to the main screen which pictured the agenda for the meeting. It was obvious his staff had done their due diligence in determining the viability of establishing a new Caribbean Major League Baseball operation. It became apparent to Bill, Bert and Phillip that their participation was not to make a pitch to the Cuban contingency. To the contrary, they were being pitched by the

Cubans who themselves wanted to be the tip of the spear that would make this new league a reality.

Bill thought to himself, "Is this really happening?" But for clarity purposes and even more so for assurances he asked Raul to reiterate his intentions and what exactly he needed from Bill's team. Raul indicated Cuba wanted to be the epicenter of the new Caribbean Major League and he wanted Bill's firm to build the entire infrastructure for the new league, including bring into the fold teams from Puerto Rico, Dominican Republic, Venezuela, and Curacao. Raul also encouraged Bill to consider having a US based team in the fold as well. All this was sweet music to Bill and his team's ear, especially the part about a US based team or teams. Bill was in total agreement. This new league had to have a US component in order to grab the attention of potential US born players and their fans. Before you knew it, Bill had a letter of understanding in his hand with a check for $100,000,000 as earnest money to begin the process.

In less than two hours, they were back in the limo and on their way back to the airport. Once back onboard Raul's Lear jet they all buckled in and popped the bottle of Cristal Champagne that Raul had graciously provided for their trip back to the States. What a day....

Chapter 22

Four Amigos Plus One

Once the Lear's landing gear lifted up, Bill's thoughts immediately shifted to the myriad of challenges his organization would face in a short period of time to establish the infrastructure for the new league. Fortunately, he was confident his dream team would be up to the challenge. All that said, Bill thought to himself he was exceedingly blessed on three fronts: his lifelong passion of establishing a new league was starting to gain momentum, couple that with the incredible news regarding his DNA discovery (life was pretty awesome) and last, but not least, he had met the love of his life in Deborah.

Bill was looking forward to his meeting with Deborah and Ramona regarding new updates on their DNA analysis. As the plane approached JFK, the runway lights glistened in the night forming a virtual tunnel on the ground directing the plane to its final landing zone. By the time the wheels touched down at 8:07 PM, Bill had already formulated his thoughts on the Why, What and How the new league would become a reality. He shared his thoughts with Phillip who he had already appointed COO of the new venture.

By 10:14 PM, Bill was on a joint conference call with Deborah and Ramona. Ramona took the lead on the call. She shared with Deborah and Bill that her forensic team had been busy. She went on to say the plant life discovery from the jersey was a species called the Rattlesnake Manna Grass. What came next sent a chill down Bill's spine. She indicated her team had determined, at one point in time, this particular plant species was native to the Providence Rhode Island area. They had narrowed the possible growth areas down to four sites, two of which currently had commercial projects erected on the sites. The remaining two sites, based on their geographic mapping analysis, still appear to be conducive to plant vegetation of some type.

Ramona went on to say without physically examining the site it would be impossible to know if the Rattlesnake Manna Grass would still be growing in the area over 130 years later. The silence on the phone at this point was deafening to the point that Ramona felt obligated to shout into the speaker, "Anybody there?" Deborah bounced back by saying, "Still trying to wrap my head around what you just said". Bill chimed in by exclaiming, "This is pretty amazing! The fact that you have the ability to analyze a small spec of plant DNA and trace it back to specific growth sites from over 130 years ago is incredible."

Then a chilling thought hit Bill like a lightning bolt. Could this plant specimen be the missing link to discovering the final resting spot of Bill's great, great-grandad Bill White. Bill broke the ice by sharing his concern, "What about the human DNA's?" Ramona was quick to point out a certain type of cadaver dog, specifically trained for forensic recovery work would be able to pick-up the scent left behind by human DNA. She added that in order to match up the scent of Bill's ancestor they would have to confiscate the Jersey from the commissioner's office. Deborah said, "Are you kidding? Is there any other way?" Ramona remarked, "Unfortunately, to the best of my knowledge, this would be the only and the best option should you they decide to move this investigation any further."

Bill asked Ramona at this point what would it take to officially move this cold case to an active investigation status. Ramona chimed in by saying the original missing person's investigation would have to be reopened under the Cold Case proviso which would entail the acquisition of a probable cause warrant to be issued by a sitting judge that would allow them to legally, (and she reiterated legally), secure the jersey from the Commissioner's office. Deborah and Bill were stunned to find themselves at this point. Deborah asked if there was a way for this to move forward without her or Bill divulging their involvement. Ramona indicated it would be highly unlikely that a sitting judge would grant a warrant without solid evidence and grounds that an actual crime had been perpetrated.

Bill cleared his throat and suggested the investigation might have to take on a more unorthodox approach? Deborah asked Bill what he had in mind. Bill asked Ramona if she had access to the jersey from Friday to Sunday evening would that give her enough time to secure a cadaver trained canine to aid in the exploration. Ramona indicated she might just have the person who would be up for the challenge. Bill asked Deborah if the projector in the commissioner's conference room had the capability to rotate and project an image on to different walls within the room. Deborah said she had seen that occur before during different meetings. Deborah, still a bit overwhelmed, chimed in by asking, "So Bill, what's your thoughts?" Bill said "Hologram." Both Deborah and Ramona were a bit surprised and asked Bill to be a bit more specific.

Ramona and Deborah were quite aware of what a hologram was, but in their minds, they wondered how this related to what they were attempting to accomplish. Bill didn't hold them in suspense much longer. Bill pointed out a prior associate of his, Helen Loo, had developed a hand size projector that could be attached magnetically to the bottom of the In- focus projector currently suspended from the center of the conference room ceiling. Her new mini projector is called the Pond. The 3D image that the Pond was capable of generating produced a resolution that is undetectable to the human eye. Bill was confident that by attaching the Pond to the bottom of the existing projector they could successfully project the life-sized 3D image of the jersey onto the exact same spot where the existing plexi-glass encased jersey resides. Deborah shared two concerns to be taken into consideration prior to embarking on any such endeavor.

One, once they had possession of the jersey it would have to be back in place in the commissioner's conference room within 48 hours; and secondly, where could they commandeer a trained cadaver dog in the New York area. Ramona was quick to point out if their research analysis was spot on, the two-day window would be sufficient, and secondly they may be in luck in securing a cadaver dog. Her good friend Max, at the NYPD canine division, had just completed a canine training session for those dogs that would be replacing some of the veteran cadaver dogs.

Max had previously introduced her to one of his prized German Shepherds named Molly who was part of the K9 team scheduled to be retired once the new class of pups had completed their training. Ramona indicated she would reach out to Max to see if he would allow Molly to join their team. Deborah suggested the window of opportunity would be in two weeks when the majority of MLB executive staff would be attending the winter owners meetings in Orlando from Wednesday to Sunday. The three of them agreed the project code name should be Manna because they would need some heavenly intervention to pull this feat off. Gaining Max's approval to allow Molly to join the team was the only item that needed to come together before the Manna project was a go. They agreed to reconvene in one week to update everyone on the status of their engagement.

First thing Monday at 8:10 AM, Ramona placed a call to Max at the NYPD canine facility. Max answered his phone on the first ring. "Maxs here." Ramona returned the pleasantry, Max, "Ramona here. How are things going in the canine world?" Max said, "No complaints." (What he was really thinking was if he did have a complaint no one would listen anyway.) Ramona asked Max how the new pups faired in their initial forensic training sessions. Max was quick to point out that with the onset of enhanced forensic technology, the new dogs' sense of smell didn't need to be as keen as the veteran dogs. In his opinion the veteran dogs had to be super sniffers.

Ramona asked when the new canine recruits were going to be pressed into service. He indicated any day now. Ramona's line of questioning then shifted to Molly's pending retirement. Max told Ramona Molly would be headed to the NYPD doggie retirement village which also served as one of the New York City rescue dog centers. Ramona asked Max if he had a moment to discuss a case that she was working on that was highly sensitive. She also asked him as a professional courtesy if he would maintain confidentially regarding the case code named Manna. Max said this hadn't come across his desk as yet. Ramona asked if he would be willing to keep this under wraps at least for now. Max said, "That depends." He indicated he wasn't interested in anything that could potentially jeopardize his pending retirement. She asked him if it were possible to have Molly join her forensic team for 48 hours. Ramona indicated this assignment would be a great way for Molly to end her illustrious career while at the same time being part of this reopening of a monumental cold case.

Max indicated it would be great for Molly to end her career on a high note but indicated he had one stipulation that he also became a part of the team as Molly's handler. Ramona was elated and reiterated to Max to please keep the lid on the Manna project for now. She indicated to him the potential timeline for the operation was within the next ten days. Max said he would wait to hear from her. Ramona immediately forwarded a text message to Bill and Deborah to share how elated she was that their team had now expanded to five with the addition of Max and Molly the cadaver dog.

Bill reached out to his good friend, Helen Loo, CEO of Waves Industries; to make arrangements to have the latest version of the Pond handheld projector delivered to his home prior to the group's scheduled follow-up meeting.

One week later at 6:10 PM, Bill opened the conference by calling roll: Deborah, "Here", Ramona, "Here", Max, "Here", Molly didn't wait to acknowledge her presence with a bark, after which Max extended her a treat. Bill acknowledged everyone's presence and asked each of them for a status update. He started off by reporting he had received the Pond projector from Helen and had already downloaded the jpeg file that Deborah sent him of the plexi-glass framed jersey as it appeared on the wall in the commissioner's conference room. He also indicated he had already conducted a test run by projecting the 3D hologram image of the jersey onto a wall in his office, was stunned by how lifelike the hologram appeared to be. He was confident that unless someone tampered with the Pond once it was secured the hologram image would be imperceptible to the human eye. Bill went on to say, "In my opinion, the image resolution is on par with any of Madame Tussaud's wax celebrity figures." The entire team was impressed with Bill's assessment.

Next, Ramona and Max chimed in with their progress update. Ramona indicated her most recent analysis of the Providence area had isolated three areas where there was still Rattlesnake Manna Grass vegetation. She felt these three areas should be the focus of their search. Max asked when Molly would get the first whiff of the jersey specimen. Deborah pointed out that she and Bill would be positioning the Pond projector in the conference room on Friday evening once the executive floor cleared out. Once the Pond initiates the 3D hologram image onto the exact spot where the jersey hung, the plexi-glass case would be removed. Bill asked if there were any additional concerns or questions. The silence on the phone was an indication, at least for now, all concerns had been addressed. Bill went on to say, "Well if there are no questions or concerns and everyone is of one accord, we should plan on rendezvousing at 6:30 AM next Saturday at the Columbus Circle parking lot top deck."

At 6:15 AM Saturday morning, Bill parked his Audi TT on the top deck of the Columbus Circle parking structure. He departed the vehicle with a box of assorted glazed and old-fashioned Dunkin Donuts and a carafe of regular coffee in hand. Bill welcomed the team, and handed over the refreshments and wished them a safe and successful trip as they prepared to depart for Providence. Deborah,

Ramona, Max and Molly climbed into the black NYPD Forensic van and off they went heading north toward Providence.

Chapter 23

Rattlesnake Manna Grass

It was now mid-afternoon, and Bill's thoughts shifted to the whereabouts of his Providence bound cohorts. Bill decided to give Deborah a call. After one ring Deborah answered the call noting her caller ID indicated Bill was on the line. Knowing how Bill was anxiously hoping to receive a progress update she immediately said they were approximately 20 miles south of Providence, but due to heavy commuter traffic going into Providence it would be at least another 40 minutes before they hit town. She indicated that the unusually heavy Saturday traffic on I-95 north heading through Greenwich, Mystic and Newport had delayed what should have been a mid-day arrival in Providence. She tried to assure him that she would keep him abreast of any and all developments as they occurred, all the while knowing she could expect to hear from Bill repeatedly throughout the day.

Bill thanked Deborah for the update. However, in an attempt to give Deborah the impression that his focus was not exclusively on their recovery mission, he went on to share with her that he and Bert had made the selections for the new CMLB league commissioner positions; and they were now in the process of extending contract offers to the respective candidates. Deborah said, "That's great news, so now what's next?" Bill was confident the candidates would accept their offers; and that being the case it was their intent to convene all the stakeholders in Cuba within the next month. "Wow" said

Deborah, "That's a pretty aggressive timeline." Bill agreed, but at the same time he knew moving the formation of the new league along expeditiously was a strategic advantage. Deborah was quick to point out to Bill not to under estimate the intel the MLB had already compiled on his new league and he shouldn't be surprised that the MLB investigation division already had comprised a fairly substantial dossier on the potential next moves the CMLB was about to undertake.

Deborah was taken aback by Bill's pronouncement that it was his intent to allow MLB the satisfaction of knowing what he wanted them to know. Deborah asked, "Why in the world would you want them to know what you have in mind?" Bill said he was counting on MLB's overreaction to ignite their political powerbase to discredit the new league. Their public skepticism would generate a hailstorm of publicity for the new league not only in the US but throughout the Caribbean. The end game would be that the new CMLB league would look to capitalize on MLB paranoia. Deborah, now having a better understanding of Bill's game plan, complimented Bill for his strategic attack on the under belly of his adversaries. Bill overheard Ramona in the background, "Hey we're coming up on check point one." Deborah said, "Duty calls. I'll get back to you a little later."

Bill turned his attention to Bert who was stunned by what he had just overheard. "Boss are you serious?" Bill asked, "About what?" "Do we really want the folks at MLB to be aware of our strategic strategy?" Bill said, "Look at it this way: we can leverage our marketing throughput by piggybacking on the MLB's public relations barrage against the new league. Bill was quick to bring to Bert's attention that the plan was to be very strategic in what propaganda they would willingly divulge for public consumption. Bill wanted Bert to know that whenever the opportunity presented itself, he wanted the new league to take advantage of the, "Other People's Money", principle (OPM). Bill smiled and Bert asked, "What's so funny?" Bill said, "It gives me great pleasure to invoke the OPM principle when it came to MLB."

Bill asked Bert when he expected to hear from their commissioner candidates. Bert indicated each offer sheet indicated a seven-day response window, and that being the case, he anticipated a favorable response. Bill charged Phillip with the task of coordinating the first CMLB summit which he hoped to hold in Cuba. Bill indicated that Cuba would be the epicenter of the new league; but in an effort to gain the greatest pre-launch hype, Miami should be the host of the first pre-summit Press Conference. He suggested Bert have Phillip work with Your Stylish Affair Group, one of the premiere event firms in the country. To their credit they had successfully orchestrated many of the most time-honored events in recent years. He stressed with Bert to make sure Phillip worked directly with Patricia Stinsome, the CEO whom he had collaborated with during the last 2016 World Games.

Bill saw a text appear on his phone from Ramona, "Nothing so far after visiting the first two sites. Only nine more to go, talk soon." Bill hadn't previously noticed the text that was now over an hour old. His anxiety was starting to get the best of him, so he decided to Face Time Deborah. She immediately appeared on his cell phone screen. Bill inquired, "What's the latest?" Deborah responded, "Nothing new as of an hour ago." Bill couldn't help but notice and hear the heavy drilling equipment in the background behind Deborah. He asked her what was going on with the big rig just to her right. Deborah said she wasn't quite sure, but it appeared the trucks were horizontally burrowing large diameter PVC tubing into the soil. She thought to herself, "ATT Uverse had finally arrived in Providence." Deborah went on to say, "Six sites down and five yet to go before night fall." Bill asked how everyone was holding up. She said Molly was doing just fine. The additional bag of doggie treats and walks through the uncharted grasslands of Providence suited her just fine. Bill said, "Ok, talk later."

Bert popped back into Bill's office to share with him that he had received, via email, affirmative responses from all four candidates. Bill was elated. "It's a go." Bert indicated he had already reached out to the event planning firm and they immediately responded with examples of the various types of social media activities they had undertaken. In addition, they provided numerous announcement paraphernalia pieces they designed for previous clients. Bert indicated that one of the pieces that got his attention was an invite piece that was designed for the Welburn Group's Holiday party which featured an envelope in the exact silhouette of the African Museum in Washington DC, where the event was to be held.

Bill received a call from Deborah at approximately 7:45 PM. It was just around dusk. She remarked it was getting dark and they would be resuming their search early tomorrow morning. Bill asked how many more sites were yet to be searched. She reported they were down to the last four. He asked Deborah how everyone was holding up and she responded that their spirits were still relatively upbeat. Bill again thanked Deborah and the entire team for their support. Bill said to Deborah on a positive note, that they had received affirmative responses from all four candidates and things were now in full swing as they prepared to pull together the press conferences that were to take place in Miami and Cuba. Bill asked if the team had made dinner plans. If not, he highly recommended the group try Kinky Monkey in the heart of downtown Newport. Deborah said she would pass the recommendation to the group.

The next morning Bill's wakeup alarm setting of 7:00 AM was preceded by a text photo featuring Deborah, Ramona and Max posed in front of one of the Planets of the Apes murals that are prominently displayed throughout the restaurant. This particular mural featured a boardroom meeting taking place with all participants being apes, both male and female, seated around a large conference table conducting business. Deborah's caption under the text photo was heartwarming, "Wishing you were here." The food and ambience were exquisite." Boy did that jump start Bill's day!

When Bill arrived at his midtown office at 8:40 AM, to his surprise, there were two newspapers positioned at his conference table. This was a bit unusual because to the best of his knowledge the firm didn't have a subscription for the New York Times or the New York Post, although he remembered there was a newsstand within walking distance of the office. As Bill was still sorting through his phone messages, Bert walked in flailing his arms and yelling "Can you believe this?" Bill asked, "Believe what?" "You obviously haven't read today's headlines," exclaimed Bert. Bill immediately picked up the Times and there it was front and center *"Caribbean MLB Coming To Save MLB. The Post* was a bit more dramatic, *MLB Move over New Sheriff in Town"*. Bert was ecstatic by what he was reading and what was being prognosticated on all the TV mainstream and sports media stations. Bill looked at Bert with a smug look that appeared as though he had just swallowed a canary.

Bert asked, "What's up?" Bill said, "I didn't think things would move this quickly, but I was pretty confident your call to Your Stylish Affair group would open the flood gates." Bert asked, "How so?" "Quite honestly, I knew if the summit proposal was leaked to the right sources it would generate a firestorm of media coverage second to none. So now you see this is the first example of how we can leverage OPM to gain relevance in the court of public opinion." The calls began to flood into the office phone bank from all over the country and the entire Caribbean corridor to the point that they had to place an extended voice message indicating that due to the high volume of calls only email communication would be responded to.

Shortly before noon, Bill decided to check in with the team. Just as he got ready to hit his automatic dial for Ramona, Deborah's number appeared on his screen. He immediately hit the accept call button. Deborah's voice was at a high-pitched level as she asked, "What have you done?" She went on to say her phone has been blowing up with calls from her office regarding the new Caribbean MLB. They wanted me and my staff to immediately develop an official positioning statement on behalf of the MLB. She said that was just the first call. The next calls came directly from the Commissioner himself. He wanted the legal department to immediately move to have the courts grant a stay to block any further action to establish their new upstart league. Deborah noticed there was complete silence on the other end of phone. She asked Bill if he was still there. "Yea, I'm here." Then it hit her. Bill was silent for another drawn out moment and Deborah went on to say, "You knew all along there would be a firestorm when the news hit the wire regarding your new league." She said, "A heads up would have been appreciated." Bill said, "And yes, I was counting on the explosive reaction in the media and in the corridors of MLB; but no I didn't want you to be blindsided. I couldn't take the chance of putting you in a compromising position by having to deny you had any advance knowledge of the launch of this new CMLB. Sometimes it's better not to know and not be called on to justify your position." Now there was utter silence on the other end. Deborah finally broke her silence by saying "I'll figure out how to deal with my folks back home."

Bill said, "On another note, what's the latest with you guys?" Deborah's sigh gave Bill the answer he was hoping not to hear. Deborah said, "There's Ramona." Bill said, "I take it things haven't gone well." Ramona acknowledged the fact that they had, unfortunately, exhausted all their probable sites and were about to make their way back to New York. Bill felt her disappointment. He thanked her and asked that she share his gratitude with the rest of the team. She said she would.

As Bill hung up, he realized his Great Great Grandad's disappearance would remain a mystery forever. Bert joined Bill in his office with a prepared press release he wanted Bill to review prior to sharing it with the various media sources. Bill took a quick glance at the document, an complimented Bert on his efforts and directed Bert to strike while the iron was hot. Bert said they had received numerous inquiries requesting Bill to appear live on radio and on-air TV programs. Bert knew Bill was a fan of Jimmy Fallon's NBC's Tonight Show, so he led off with that request first. As Bert was contemplating the thought of appearing on the Jimmy Fallon Show, he noticed his phone, which he had placed on vibrate, was about to bounce off his desk. He noticed Ramona's name pop up on the screen. He hit the accept button and at first, he heard an inaudible sound that he could hardly make out. A second later Ramona screamed out "We have a hit." Bill said, "Come again." "Yes, we were headed out of town and Molly went berserk when we were passing an ATT Universe dig site that had shut down for the day. We immediately pulled over and let Molly and Max out at the site. Molly went into a frenzy barking and digging away at the site.

Max was quick to grab Molly's collar and pulled her over to get a fresh whiff of the jersey. Molly seemed to go into an even greater frenzy then, digging feverishly with her paws. Max yelled at me saying, "We definitely have a hit." Ramona jumped out the truck with a reel of yellow emergency tape and wire stakes then began to cordon off the area. Bill asked Deborah to call 911 and get the proper authorities out to the scene. Deborah did so and within minutes had both an EMS truck and a Providence Police car flashing their bright red and blue emergency lights. Ramona and Max showed their NYPD Badges and shared with them the essence of their search. With the help of the EMS, Police and the two shovels they brought with them, they were able to unearth almost as much as a three-foot-long and four foot deep hole at the site. Then suddenly Bill heard a scream in the background, "It's a bone and skull." Everybody stopped digging and began to drop to their knees and started to dig gingerly with their hands. Bill screamed back in the phone "Did you say bone and skull?" That's when the call dropped off because Bill's cell phone ran out of juice.

Ten minutes later Bill's phone was sufficiently charged to call Deborah back. Bill could hardly discern Deborah's voice. There seemed to be a lot more people at the site. She switched off her speaker mode and Bill could all of a sudden hear her perfectly. Bill asked what was going on. She was quick to note, in addition to the EMS and Police vehicles, there were now two TV trucks and two local radio station vehicles on sight. She said so far, they had recovered two leg bones and a partial skull. Darkness had begun to settle in, and they decided to shut down the site until sunrise. Bill could tell in Deborah's voice she was totally exhausted from this unbelievable discovery.

Chapter 24
Caribbean MLB To Be or Not To Be

In spite of all the excitement, Deborah realized Ramona, Max and Molly would be required to remain in Providence to coordinate the dig and she would need to make arrangements for her return trip to New York. Her only option was to use mass transit in order to arrive in a timely fashion for her scheduled rendezvous with Bill. The Amtrak Northern Red line was the only viable mode of transportation that traveled twice a day between Maine and New York Penn Station. The timing of Deborah's return was critical because the jersey had to be repositioned back in the Commissioner's office by late Sunday evening prior to Sherm's scheduled janitorial service in the building. Deborah gave Ramona and Max a hug and patted Molly on her head as she jumped into her Uber car heading to the Providence Amtrak train station.

Bill anxiously awaited Deborah's return as he stood at the end of Penn Station's track 7 with a tall of sack of **Nathans Coney Island hot dogs** in hand. The 9:45 Northern Red line rolled into Penn Station. As Deborah made her way off the second car, Bill extended *the Nathans* bag and said, "Dinner's on me." Deborah said, tongue and cheek, "You shouldn't have." Deborah came close and gave Bill a nice hug while whispering in his ear, "We did it. Bill White is no longer an unsolved cold case." Bill didn't want their hug to end. When they separated, Deborah noticed a slight tear in Bill's right eye. Bill asked Deborah if she had the jersey. She said, "Are you kidding?

By all means." Bill smugly said, "I would think it needs to be steam pressed before we place it back in the case. I suggest we go back to my apartment and get that handled." Deborah said, "You can do better than that. Trying to get a girl up to your apartment to steam a shirt is a bit lame." Bill teased, "Well, do you have a better idea?" Deborah responded playfully, "Yes I do. I have a stand-up steamer in my office closet." "Well let's do this." They departed the terminal, on to Lexington Avenue and hailed a taxi heading to 245 Park Ave.

Once in the building they headed directly to the 6th floor where Deborah removed the stand-up steamer from her closet and filled the reservoir with two cups of water while Bill stood on a step stool and repositioned the surveillance camera. He removed the Pond projector which immediately stopped projecting the 3D encased jersey image. Deborah completed steaming the jersey and she and Bill repositioned the jersey in its case and placed the case back in its original location on the wall. They turned off the lights and departed the building. Once out on to Park Avenue they made their way down Park Avenue. Deborah and Bill were waiting for the traffic light to change at the corner of Park and Lexington when all of a sudden Sherm's janitorial van passes them on their immediate left. Deborah thought to herself any delay on their part could have spelled disaster.

Bill asked Deborah if he could interest her in a nightcap. She graciously declined, saying, "It's been a long day, but a great day. I'd like to take a rain check." Bill was quick to point out he would hold her to it. With a smile, Deborah said, "I have no doubt you will." With that, Bill hailed a taxi for Deborah. As he opened the door of the taxi, he planted a brotherly kiss on her right cheek and sent her on her way.

By 6:30 AM the next morning, Deborah had completed MLB's official position statement and placed it on Lynn's desk outside the Commissioner's office. Her real thoughts, however, were focused on the forensic dig taking place in Providence. Her thoughts were interrupted when her cell phone id showed Ramona calling. As she hit accept, Ramona's voice on the other end was emotionally charged when she blurted out, "Our John Doe is no longer. We are now in possession of two cadaver femur bones and a partial cranium." Ramona went on to say, "I don't need to tell you it's been an exhausting four days but without a doubt it has been the most rewarding experience I've had in my entire 30-year career. We can all feel proud that we accomplished what we set out to do. This entire experience has been so surreal. Just think, having the opportunity to shine a light on an injustice, and right a wrong that's been allowed to go unchallenged for over 140 years is something special. Girl we did it. Thanks for letting me be a part of something so life changing."

Deborah, it's your call. Where do we go from here? Understand we are at the point where we will now have to expose our clandestine activities in order to officially open our cold case with the FBI and NYPD. And of course, that would include exposing the alleged involvement of the commissioner's ancestors." Deborah asked Ramona how long she could keep the identity of the remains under wraps. Ramona said she wasn't sure, but 2-3 weeks based on the condition of the remains. Deborah said, "I'll take it. In the interim, let's make sure Max and Bill keep things under wraps until we give them the go ahead. Rest assured in the end that I'm committed to seeing that our ball player receives his long overdue memorial service." Deborah questioned Ramona about how she planned to proceed to unravel the sordid details of what they sensed occurred to cause the brutal death of Bill White in 1879.

Ramona indicated to Deborah that until they completed their forensic investigation, then and only then, would they approach the Commissioner and divulge all their circumstantial evidence that points directly to his ancestors as potential perpetrators of this heinous crime. How the Commissioner chooses to spin this cold case in the court of public opinion would be up to him. It wouldn't surprise me if he chose to be dismissive of all the scientific proof as fake news and flat out deny any and all involvement of his ancestors. So, for right now, let's keep a close eye on how things play out once the New York media begins to take an interest in how this cold case resurfaced after over 140 years.

"For now, Ramona, I recommend you get some rest and we get back together for lunch in a couple of days." Ramona said, "I'm all for that; and by the way you may want to invite Bill to join us for lunch on Thursday." Deborah said she would contact Bill shortly to give him an update.

Deborah decided to take Bill up on his dinner offer. Instead of having dinner at his place, however, she decided to switch the script and invite him over to her apartment, located on the upper east side of Harlem. Not one skilled in the culinary arts, Deborah decided to order out from Victors Café on 52nd right off of Broadway. Victors Cafe was known for their two signature dishes, Paella and Empanadas. She was confident Bill would enjoy the selections. First things first. She needed to reach out to Bill to see if he was a go and if so, she would dispatch her Uber driver to swing by Victors Café prior to picking her up at her office.

She hit Bill's number on her automatic dial and as usual Bill picked up after the first ring. Bill asked Deborah how her day had been so far? Deborah responded, "Well, once I got through the fire storm your new league pronouncement generated, I was ok. The overall hysteria seems to be growing exponentially." She knew by Bill's silence he was feeling pretty confident. He had accomplished his first hurdle by generating a media frenzy that appeared to have no end in sight. She made it clear she wanted to take Bill up on his offer to have dinner, without hesitation, Bill said, "Yes, where should we meet?" When she told him her apartment, he was pleasantly surprised. "What time and where is your apartment?" She responded, "7 PM" and gave him the address. He confirmed that her apartment was in the shadows of the Apollo Theater and asked what he could bring. She suggested that if he had a special wine he enjoyed, he should feel free to bring it along.

Bill told Deborah that a good friend and classmate, Billie Miles, had become a vintner in the Napa Valley and was producing a non-Oak Chardonnay, called Kopriva. "I'll bring two bottles just in case you want to start your own Kopriva fan club." Deborah said, "See you at 7 PM." After hanging up Bill felt as if the entire dinner invite interchange had the feeling of a corporate bilateral summit gathering. Quite honestly, though, he was elated to be in Deborah's company anytime and place.

At 5:15 PM, Deborah was out front at 245 Park Avenue awaiting her Uber car which pulled up to the curb moments later. Her female driver introduced herself as Gabby as she opened the door of the Cadillac X5. Deborah slid in the rear seat with briefcase in hand. Once back in the driver's seat, Gabby asked Deborah what smelled so good in the Victors' bag? Deborah answered, "Victors' world-renowned Paella and Empanadas taste as good as they smell." When Gabby pulled up to Deborah's apartment, she helped carry the sizable Victors' bag up to Deborah's ground floor apartment. Deborah reached into her purse and pulled out a $25 Victors' Café gift card and gave it to Gabby. Needless to say, Gabby was taken aback by Deborah's generosity and said with an advance notice she would make herself available whenever Deborah required transportation. Deborah said she would keep that in mind. Deborah headed inside where she began to freshen up for her arriving guest.

Bill's Audi *tt* pulled up curbside at Deborah's apartment promptly at 6:55 PM. He reached over to the passenger seat and lifted up a large bouquet of colorful spring flowers and two individual bags containing the bottles of Kopriva he promised. Bill quickly headed to the front door where he rang the doorbell and within moments Deborah opened the right side of the double ornate metal lead glass door. She was wearing a stunning black jump suit with a striking gold African necklace.

Bill leaned forward and planted a brotherly kiss on her right cheek and handed her the bouquet of flowers. She smiled, "How sweet. I've got the perfect vase. Please come in." Once inside, Bill asked where he should put the bottles of wine. Deborah pointed to a gray ceramic cylinder that appeared to have been chilled. Bill asked, "Deborah what was that great smell coming from the kitchen?" Deborah said, "Paella and Empanadas, courtesy of Victors Café". Bill asked if he could uncork the Kopriva and Deborah responded, "Please do so." Deborah had already set the dining room table and she was now ready to remove the entre from the warming oven. Bill poured a half full glass of wine for each of them and handed Deborah a glass. He lifted his glass and proposed a toast. To good friends and the best of times; and they clinked their glasses. After taking a sip, Deborah smiled and said, "Wow this Kopriva is quite smooth and yet crisp." Bill was glad she approved. Deborah said, "How about dinner?" Bill said, "How did you know Paella is my all-time favorite dish?" He assisted her as she sat down, sliding her chair forward. Bill asked if he could bless the food. "Please do the honors." Bill bowed his head and said, "Bless the food before us, the friends beside us, and the love between us." Deborah thought to herself, "This guy obviously knows the Lord." Bill practically inhaled his food. He complemented Deborah on her choice of restaurants and menu. "I'm glad you enjoyed everything." Bill said, "Victors Café will go to the top of my list of favorite restaurants."

Deborah asked Bill if he was a music fan. "Smooth Jazz, "He answered," mostly Brian Culberson, Gerald Albright, Kirk Waylon, Dee Lucas, Boney James and Jonathan Butler are my top guys." Deborah said, "Brian's Funk album was one of my all-time favorites." Bill thought to himself, "This lady is special, not only does she have exquisite taste in food, but she also has a sophisticated appetite for good music." As the evening drew to an end, Bill thanked Deborah for an unforgettable evening of food and music. He asked if he could call on her again. She said she would like that. Bill moved closer, and this time he embraced her in his arms and gave her a passionate kiss that he had fantasized about from the very first time he laid eyes on her. As Deborah opened her eyes, she thought to herself, "This guy is hot, and boy is he a good kisser." As she escorted him to the door, she knew in her heart this was the guy she had been waiting for. Her knight in shining armor fired up the Audi *tt* engine and sped south on 125th street. She could barely discern the sound of her heartbeat over the oscillating sound of his Audi *tt* engine as it roared in the distance.

As Bill headed back to Manhattan, he could only think about how beautiful and special the evening had been. Of course, the thought occurred to him that they hadn't even discussed any MLB or forensic happenings during their entire evening.

Chapter 25

Four Commissioners Step to the Plate

June 22, 2020

Just as Bill was making his way down the East Side highway in bumper to bumper traffic and not able to get his Audi *tt* out of second gear, his cell phone pinged alerting him Bert was calling. He answered after one ring and says, "What's up?" Bert enthusiastically responded that business was picking up and things were moving at hyper speed. We are getting call backs from some of the most talented baseball people in the country wanting to be part of our new league. Bill was not stunned that the word was out regarding their upstart league. Bert suggested they get together ASAP to discuss how they wanted to position themselves to these prospective candidates and possible MLB insiders that were by now intently monitoring their activities. Bill agreed to meet with Bert within the hour at their mid-town office.

By the time Bill arrived at the office Bert had assembled a stack of resumes that had been faxed into their office within the last 24 hours. It was obvious as Bill made a cursory inspection of the resumes that the interest level of the proposed new league had grabbed the attention of some of the most notable baseball people here in the US and in the Caribbean international community. Bill suggested to Bert that they settle down and work through the stack. Bill asked Rose, his administrative assistant, to put on a fresh pot of coffee because he and

Bert would be doing an old-fashioned all-nighter. Bert suggested they begin evaluating the resumes by separating them into three stacks. One stack would be designated as possible candidates with baseball pedigree, two for possible candidates with no baseball but with other sports related experience and the third stack for those that were not suited for further consideration. At about 1 AM they had finished filtering the entire stack of resumes of which many of them ended up in the third group of undesirables. Fortunately, they ended up with 15 stellar resumes that survived the first cut. Bill assigned Bert the task of whittling down the 15 resumes to the final 8 candidates by AM the next day. Bert nodded his head and said, "I guess an all-nighter is the order of the day. Bill suggested they reconvene at 10 AM sharp. Bert was quick to say, "You mean in nine hours?" Bill didn't hesitate to remind Bert that it was his idea that they whittle down the list of potential candidates ASAP.

Bill arrived back at the office at 9:58 AM sharp with two cups of Starbucks double Latte Macchiatos in hand. Bert was still sitting in the chair Bill had left him in some nine hours earlier. He raised his head from the desk and his blood shot eyes were hidden behind his Persol aviator sunglasses. Bill, seeing Bert said to him, "You look like death warmed over." Bert said, "It's good to see someone got a sense of humor. That being said, "The late night paid off." He went on to say the final 8 candidates he is prepared to present all have extraordinarily high baseball IQ's with incredible pedigrees. "Ok, let's see what you've got." "My first two commissioner nominees are Joshua Vincent and Tres Rodriguez.

Joshua Vincent is a prominent member of the Cuban Baseball Federation who was the mastermind behind all of Cuba's International baseball operations. Tres Rodriquez is currently the Dominican Republic Sports Director who directed all International and World Game competition, not only for baseball but also basketball and track and field. I'm confident these two individuals will provide the leadership we need for our Caribbean platform." Bill said, "pretty impressive." Bert went on to say, "It only gets better. I'm recommending we have one commissioner oversee both the Puerto Rican and Curasol contingency. My nominee is Hall of Famer, Jose Perez who for the last ten years has played a major role in the rehabilitation of both Puerto Rican and Curacao international baseball operations since the devastating hurricane in 2016. And finally, our first female commissioner is Dorthey Jeaneo, Olympic Baseball Gold Medalist and most recent United States Senior Director of Health and Education in the Obama administration. Her experience as both an athlete and statesperson will serve us well as she maneuvers her way through the political maze in the Miami community." Bill was in total agreement with Bert's recommendation and says, "Sweet, I like it. Great job." Bill suggested they consider offering the remaining four finalists' positions within their CMLB administration. Bert said, "Sounds great."

Bill continued, "Now, comes the hard part." Bert rolled back in his chair and said to himself… "What now?" Bill took on a persona that gave the appearance he was having an out of body transformation as he began to share his thoughts with Bert by speaking in the third person.

"Bill knows who needs to lead the charge… Yea Bill knows it's got to be Bill. Bill's been groomed for this his entire life. Bill, you the man. Bill it's your time to shine. Let's do it." Bert was stunned by what he just observed. He had heard of people like Ricky Henderson who frequently referred to themselves in the 3rd person but this display coming from Bill caught him completely off guard. Bert realized Bill had a tremendous amount of pressure resting on his shoulders but still the whole experience kinda freaked him out. Fortunately, in a matter of seconds Bill was back to his normal self and picked up their conversation right where they were before Bill's paranormal outburst. Bert had no doubt Bill had what it took to bring his lifelong dream to launch a new professional baseball league that would rival MLB to fruition. He knew the dream team Bill had assembled had the utmost confidence in his ability to accomplish the task. Bert took advantage of the moment and said, "I agree with both Bills, count me in."

The first order of business was to extend contract offers to their targeted candidates. Simultaneously Bill indicated he would begin the process to solidify the new leagues' financial foundation. His first consultation for funding would be the International Sports Betting Authority. In light of the 2018 Supreme Court decision ruling that each individual state has the ability to institute sports betting, his first consultation for funding for the new league would be with the respective Sports Betting Authorities in each state and Caribbean Island. His plan was to couple the sports betting consortium with a robust domestic and international commercial sponsorship platform as the financial pillars of the new league. Prior to the Supreme Court groundbreaking decision, Nevada was the only state that was able to legally conduct sports betting throughout the United States. Now after three years, each professional league has generously benefited from their 2% stake from betting line revenues. In addition, Bill always wanted to have a charitable component to his new league that would be committed to reinvest in each team's respective communities. The new league 501(c)(3) charitable status would be similar to that of the PGA and LPGA. Bill knew this type of commitment would not only resonate in the communities where the teams existed but would have far reaching impact in the court of public opinion. And the fact that MLB had abandoned their charitable status some time ago would further bolster the new league's gravitas as a caring organization.

Bill was confident the new league's fundamental business model would enable it to attract quality team owners, high end corporate sponsors, and most of all gain the interest of front line major league players who were willing to jump to the new league. Bill knew just the person he could call on to oversee the financial foundation activities, his good friend and the most recent Secretary of Commerce and prior CEO of Bank of America, Noel Leon.

Chapter 26

New Sheriff in Town

August 1, 2020

Bill and Bert arrived early at the La Guardia executive air terminal to board their scheduled 8 AM charter flight to Miami. Typically, they would be traveling on Southwest with other staff members, but on this occasion their entire staff had traveled to Miami three days earlier to ensure that all the arrangements were in place to facilitate the arrival of the Cuban, Dominican, Puerto Rican, Curacao and Venezuelan delegations. If all went as planned, this meeting would serve as the official public launch of the new Caribbean MLB. The plane touched down in Miami in less than two hours. They climbed into the Escalade and were whisked off to the Fountain Blue Hotel where the first general session of the Caribbean MLB was to take place. Both Bill and Bert noticed how few cars were traveling southbound on inter-state Highway 95 at a time of day that usually experienced bumper to bumper grid lock traffic.

Once across the Key Biscayne causeway they noticed this huge sea of humanity waving flags and banners of what appeared to be Cuban, Dominican, Puerto Rican, Curacao and Venezuelan representing the respective countries that would be the footprint of the new league. The entire scene appeared to have the flavor of a World Cup International event. Both Bill and Bert thought to themselves, this was exactly the type of hype and energy they wanted their new league to generate. They couldn't believe what they were witnessing. The nationalistic pride that was on display was mind blowing. As the Escalade pulled into the parking lot, they noticed several food trucks, open pit grills with huge tempura skillets filled with seafood paella and even a giant revolving spit with glistening coals where a full-size pig hung. There was no doubt a festival of grand proportions had erupted. Every television network truck was lined up on the side of the road. Bill's advance team had delivered beyond his expectations.

Reality was beginning to set in. Bill was convinced that this entire scene provided a clear indication that the Latin influence on the new league would be profound. The style of play and fan enthusiasm would definitely be a breath of fresh air to the baseball community. Bill was convinced the economic impact throughout the Caribbean region would be astronomical. Miami with its diverse influx of Caribbean cultures would also be in an ideal position to benefit economically from the new league's presence.

As Bill and Bert worked their way through the crowd into the hotel foyer, they encountered more fanatical fans in full party mode that appeared to permeate the entire hotel. Multiple steel drum bands serenaded the overflow hordes of people lining the hotel corridors. They finally made their way to the ballroom where their session was scheduled to begin within the hour. As the door opened, they were blown away by the sheer number of people, all appearing to be cheering in appreciation for the triumphant return of Major League Baseball to the field, after a year and one half of deep division between the owners and players' union. Thank goodness it would be the CMLB that would be filling the void. Bill honestly had not anticipated this type of hero's welcome, but he fantasized this was exactly what would happen. This display of enthusiasm was music to his and all his stakeholders' in attendance ears.

The media contingency appeared to be taken aback by what they were seeing. The fact that the usual sports reporters were joined by their fellow network news anchors to cover an event was an acknowledgement that this new league could potentially change the landscape of not only the American baseball scene but the entire international sports scene.

As Bill made his way to the podium, he thought to himself that this type of pageantry was usually reserved for Super Bowl and World Cup stages. The music in the auditorium was pulsating with the sound of Tina Turner's classic tune "Simply the Best." He couldn't help but notice the giant screens positioned on both sides of the stage blasting off pyrotechnics highlighting the message "CMLB The Players League." The opening slide captured the true essence of what the new league was all about, "The Players League." Bill momentarily reflected on how proud his Great Great Grandad would be to see his legacy as the driving force behind the creation of a new league where players are equity partners. This could become the greatest coup d'état in the last 200 years of sports history.

As Bill acknowledged the applause and chants from the audience, which seemed to resonate more loudly with every passing moment, he asked his entire team, seated in the front row, to stand and acknowledge the appreciation. Bill couldn't help but reflect on all the support he had received over the years to bring him to this point in time where the entire sports world was pre-occupied with what he was about to share with the audience. As he took note of his prepared remarks, pictured on both teleprompter screens, he glanced down at the standing room only crowd and began by saying, "I'd like to share with all of you why I feel I'm the luckiest guy on this side of heaven. First, I'd like to thank my Great Great Grandad Bill White who just happened to be the first bi-racial Major League Baseball player to play in an official MLB league game for the Providence Grays in 1879." Bill gestured up to sky and said for all to hear… "Granddad, I know you are smiling down on us with your approval. Hopefully there's baseball in heaven."

Bill went on to delineate why the CMLB will be the gold standard for all professional major league operations. He continued to share in great detail the unique business model that would position the CMLB as one of the premiere sports organizations in the world. Bill made it perfectly clear the CMLB would be deeply rooted in the communities they served. He also clarified that the league's 501(c)(3) status would bolster their ability to provide charitable contributions to many of those regions that had recently experienced devastating hurricanes. Bill knew he had struck the right chord because his next statement brought the audience to their feet. He announced that each player would be offered an equity ownership position in the new league. And if that wasn't enough, he delivered what would be the crown jewel for the new league. "Thanks to the United States Supreme Court's 2018 decision which allowed sports betting on a state by state basis, the new league's financial underpinnings would be derived from revenues generated from the sports betting lines in the United States and each of the participating team's countries."

While Bill was the center of attention, little did he know MLB had positioned one of their own in the audience equipped with a hidden camera that was streaming live video back to the Commissioner's conference room where the Commissioner and his entire staff, including Deborah, were intently observing. As they watched, the silence in the Commissioner's conference room was deafening. The Commissioner broke the silence by saying, "F**k these guys, we will bury them. Starting right now." He directed Deborah to pull together a confidential brief for the owners' review, recommending they engage all the resources at their disposal to crush this upstart league before their inaugural season. Deborah was stunned by the Commissioner's directive. She asked him, "Isn't this something you might want to take to the owners for their buy-in?" Jake abruptly said, "This shit ain't gonna happen on my watch." The Commissioner was quick to continue with, "Enough conversation. I want to see a draft of this brief on my desk before the close of business today. Is that understood?"

Chapter 27

Let' em Eat Cake

Deborah wasn't totally surprised when she received an action required email from Lynn that night announcing a leadership staff meeting in the Commissioner's conference room at 8 AM sharp, attendance mandatory. What got her attention was the emphasis on mandatory attendance required. She was well aware of the Commissioner's obsession to crush the upstart CMLB league.

Deborah arrived at 245 Park Ave. by 7:30 AM and made a quick stop in her office to check her phone for voice messages. Just as she was about to walk out of her office, she pulled out her iPhone 12 to turn on the utility voice memos application and then made her way down the corridor to the 8:00 AM, all hands on deck, session. She took her usual seat, on the opposite side of the conference table, directly across from where the Commissioner typically sat. At 7:55 AM, the Commissioner arrived with coffee in hand. He announced to the group that after due deliberation and consultation with key owners and stakeholders, he would recommend that the owner's executive committee allow the CMLB to move forward with their abbreviated inaugural season.

Deborah couldn't believe what she had just heard. Her initial thought, "Was who did the Commissioner collaborate with to arrive at what appeared, on the surface, to be a complete reversal of where his mindset was the day before." Once Jake opened the meeting up for questions, it immediately became apparent which owners he had included in his inner circle. Those select owners just happened to be the teams that had the highest player payroll. It was evident the Commissioner had convinced the owners he collaborated with that the new league and it was destined to go bust after the first season. In his opinion, those high payroll players would now become available at substantially reduced salaries. It was apparent the overriding rationale to allow the new league to move forward was greed on the part of select owners. If one could read Deborah's mind you would see that she was well aware that most decisions the Commissioner made were calculated to maintain, at all cost, the prevailing dominance of the major market teams to the detriment of the small market teams. Without a doubt his mantra was to keep the big boys happy and knowingly allow the small market teams to get screwed.

When the Commissioner concluded the meeting, he asked Deborah to take the lead in working with the Public Relations staff to pull together the media release announcing MLB's official position on the CMLB announcement. He punctuated his statement by saying, "Have it on my desk today by the close of business." Deborah indicated she would be heading directly over to the PR department's office, located on the 5th floor, once she retrieved some of her notes from her office. Once back in her office, she reached for her phone and clicked off the utilities voice memos icon. She immediately contacted Bill via her private cell phone and, as always, Bill answered on the first ring. Bill's usual opening line when speaking to Deborah was "Hello Ms. Deborah. How is your day going?" In a slightly muffled voice, Deborah responded by facetiously saying, "Oh my day is off to a robust start. By the way do you have any plans for lunch today?" Bill responded, "For you, lunch would be just fine." Deborah said, "Great! Let's meet at Dumbo underneath the Brooklyn Bridge? How's one o'clock works for you?" "Sounds great, see you soon." Just as Bill was about to jettison out of his office to meet Deborah for lunch, Bert peeked into his office to see if there was any update from Deborah.

Bill reached back to grab his phone and as he passed Bert on his way out, said, "Nothing as of yet, but hopefully over lunch, Deborah will have something to pass along." Bill's Uber driver awaited his arrival. Once Bill exited the building his Uber driver opened the rear passenger door; and off they went, heading toward the Brooklyn Bridge. They arrived at Dumbo within minutes. Bill's feelings for Deborah, now more than ever, were starting to be consumed by his hormonal instincts to be with her whenever the opportunity presented itself. He realized he was physically attracted to her from the very first time they met at MLB headquarters. As the Uber driver pulled up to the valet station in front of Dumbo, he immediately got a glimpse of Deborah sitting at the outdoor café sipping, a café Latte.

Bill instructed the driver to drop him off and if possible be on call to return in two hours. He immediately joined Deborah at her table. They exchanged hugs and Bill's thoughts flashed to when he might have Deborah back in his arms in a more intimate setting. Deborah had taken it upon herself to order Bill's favorite drink, a non-alcoholic Arnold Palmer. Deborah could tell by Bill's body language that he was anxious to hear how things were going back at MLB headquarters. Bill broke the ice by asking Deborah how her session had gone this morning. Deborah asked Bill if he had a set of ear buds in his bag. Bill said, "I think I do." Deborah removed her phone from her purse and placed it on the table. She directed Bill to connect his ear buds to her phone.

As Bill plugged his ear buds into Deborah's iPhone, he noticed Deborah had already activated the phone's utility voice memo tab. What he heard next blew him away. Deborah could tell by Bill's expression he was somewhat puzzled by what he had just heard. Bill was smiling and shaking his head at the same time as he removed the ear buds. His comment said it all. "This guy is true to form… he is truly the ass hole he appears to be. So, he thinks if he throws us a bone we'll just fade away. His privileged self-serving attitude "Let' em Eat Cake for tomorrow they die seemed to be his rallying call. With all we have accomplished in such a short period of time, he still believes the CMLB is just a flash in the pan group of amateurs trying to compete with the big boys. The day of reckoning is close at hand." Bill shared with Deborah that the CMLB would be turning up the heat when their national business conference call to all their stakeholders takes place, to announce their six major international sponsors. This national business conference call will be simultaneously streamed both domestically and internationally. He warned her if she thought the commissioner's defiance was running at an all-time high, she hadn't seen anything yet because once the word got out regarding the CMLB's premiere sponsorships and television network alliances his paranoia would undoubtedly escalate to new heights. Deborah noticed Bill still had that quizzical look on his face. She told him it appeared he was somewhat conflicted by the Commissioner's course of action. He confided in Deborah, as disturbed as he was regarding the Commissioner's tactics, he wasn't going to lose sight of the fact that he was looking a gift horse in the mouth when it came to the MLB decision to allow the upstart CMLB league to move forward.

Deborah reminded Bill that this Commissioner's past inconsistent behavior dictates he could flip flop overnight. So, she encouraged him to move forward post haste. Whatever it was that she said, it caused Bill to instantly switch gears. Bill, unconsciously and with little hesitation, asked Deborah "What about us?" Deborah was taken aback by the question which seemed to come out of nowhere. But Deborah knew she also had begun to have those same thoughts about Bill.

She gathered her wits and calmly told Bill now wasn't the time for them to begin a romantic relationship. Even though this wasn't the response he hoped for, Bill, was encouraged by Deborah's response, he responded, "So you are saying there will come a time." Deborah looked into his eyes and rested her hand on his and said, "I would like for there to be a time."

Chapter 28

Now or Never

Deborah texted Bill requesting he meet her at Havana Central at 7 PM. Bill glanced down at his phone only to see Deborah's text as he and Bert were about to leave the office at 4:23 PM. Bill could only speculate what could be so important that Deborah wanted to rendezvous so soon on the heels of his ground-breaking Miami conference. His first thought was that it was going to be a tight timeline. He decided right then and there that he would do whatever it took to make their meeting back in Manhattan.

Prior to departing from the hotel, Bill and Bert had already inked the new league's first promotional contract for the naming rights for all six CMLB stadiums. This initial deal all but guaranteed the CMLB first season would be financially solid in the black. Bill pointed out to Bert that next challenge was to start an aggressive player and coach recruitment process. Unbeknownst to Bill, Bert had already taken the lead by initiating exploratory discussions with a highly respected general manager who had recently resigned his position with the Marlins once their new ownership group was in place. Initially, Ozzie Samuels was on the initial list of prospective commissioners, but he missed the cut for one of the four commissioner positions.

Bert indicated he had reached out to Ozzie to determine his interest in becoming the new league's Vice President in charge of player and coach recruitment. Ozzie had already distinguished himself as one of the nation's top baseball recruiters and talent scouts. In addition, he was the chief architect behind the Gold Medal winning 2020 USA Olympic Baseball team. If you could read Bert's thoughts, you would know that in Bert's mind it was a foregone conclusion that Ozzie was his choice for the job.

Once airborne, Bill heard his phone ping indicating another message from Deborah saying, "All hell breaking loose back here. See you at 7PM. Oh, by the way I've asked Ramona to join us". Bill wasn't surprised by the hysteria being generated at MLB and quite honestly, he loved it.

At 6:05 PM the private Net Jet Lear pulled into the private executive hanger where Bill and Bert immediately climbed into an Uber Suburban. Off they went heading towards their 7:00 PM rendezvous with Deborah and Ramona. When they arrived at Havana Central slightly before 7, they were greeted by the maitre d. Bill took the liberty of requesting a quiet booth in the rear of the restaurant. Bill asked the maitre d if Deborah Robinson had arrived as yet, and he replied, "Not as yet," with that, Bill and Bert headed off to the bar. At 7:15 PM Deborah and Ramona entered the restaurant. Bill immediately noticed their arrival but as they rose Bert said "Woe, who's who?" Bill then realized Bert hadn't met either of them. Bill said, "Hold on, Deborah is my special friend." And Bert said, "Well is Ms. Ramona spoken for?" Bill said, "I have no idea, but just remember we are here on business." Bert said, "There's nothing wrong with combining a little pleasure with business."

They departed the bar to meet Deborah and Ramona at the maître d's stand. After Bill introduced Bert to both of them, they were escorted to their booth. Their waiter immediately greeted them and noticed Bill and Bert had brought their drinks from the bar. He commented, "It looks like you guys have got a jump start on the ladies, so I'll start with them. Ladies what can we get you from the bar?" Deborah responded by saying, "A glass of Kopriva non-oak Chardonnay," and Ramona chimed in saying, "That sounds interesting, I'll have the same."

Both Deborah and Ramona wondered to themselves why Bill decided to have Bert join them for dinner. Not knowing, Bill thought to himself, I guess they are probably wondering why Bert is here. So, he decided to clear the air. Bill said, "I asked Bert to join us because I believed it was time he was made aware of what we have been up to." You could see the stunned look not only on Bert's face, but also the same quizzical look was inescapable on both Deborah's and Ramona's faces. If you could put that look into words, it would be "Why now?" Bill went on to explain.

The relationships Bert has nurtured with our international and domestic partners may be impacted by what we decide to share for public consumption. Ramona chimed in saying, "We are now at that crossroad." She went on to say, "We now have conclusive proof that the remains of our John Doe are in fact Bill White's. The look on Bert's face went from stunned to outright shock. Ramona didn't stop there. She went on to say, "The two other DNA specimens can now be confirmed to be direct ancestors of Jake and Bill." Bert could no longer maintain his silence as he asked, "What in the world is going on?" Deborah decided it would be best to bring Bert up to speed. She shared with him the story from the start with her great grandfather's interaction with the mixed race Brown University baseball player who actually played in a Major League baseball game in 1879 and then mysteriously turned up missing, never to be heard from again until now. Bert jumped in, "So, you are saying these remains are this kid's?" Ramona said, "Without a doubt." Deborah continued, "It gets better." She said, "When she came on staff as MLB's Chief Legal Counsel, she really hadn't paid a lot of attention to the baseball Jersey that was prominently displayed in the Vice Commissioner's office."

It wasn't until the Commissioner decided to freak out by exposing himself, figuratively and literally, for who he really is as a person that I decided not to get mad but get even. Initially I was so pissed, I wanted to go into his conference room with a baseball bat and beat the hell out of him and the prized memorabilia in his office, the Providence Grays jersey. Then one night, out of nowhere, during one of my dreams, I reflected on the story my Mom shared with me regarding my great Grandpa, Moncalm Robinson. He described in great detail the baseball jersey the college player wore in the game and how he made a gift of the jersey to the kid before he left the club house. I realized the jersey he described could actually be the one encased in the Commissioner's office. That's when I decided to reach out to my good friend Ramona, who happens to be the NYPD Chief Director of Forensics. I won't bore you with all the details." Bert said, "Rest assured, boring this is not. Actually, I'm flat blown away by what I've heard so far. But I do have a question. Where do Bill and I fit into this saga?"

Deborah picked back up where she left off by saying, "Bill's connection came about purely by accident. When we were attempting to collect a specimen of the Commissioner's DNA, Bill's coffee cup was mistakenly collected along with the Commissioner's cup and both were sent off for analysis. To say the least, we were all shocked when the results came in. Now as to how our team, which included our own canine specialist, recovered the remains of our ball player, I'll save you the details; but needless to say, God has had his hand in the mix right from the beginning." Bert, still reeling from all he had just heard hadn't paid attention when Bill asked, "Where are we going from here?" Deborah said, "We may be getting a little ahead of ourselves. There is an elephant in the room, and, in light of that fact, all hell has broken loose at MLB and the Commissioner is on a rampage.

My legal brief, which stated that the MLB didn't have any legal standing to secure an injunction against the new CMLB, didn't help to improve his mood. She went on to direct her comments to both Bill and Bert when she pointed out that the Commissioner was waffling on whether or not he was willing to accept the advice he received from his inner circle of large market owners or would he seek injunctions to hopefully disrupt the launch of the new CMLB league and ultimately crush you guys. Bill said to Deborah, "It's not surprising; this guy is so short sighted and consumed with greed and power that he can't see that both the CMLB and MLB can thrive and co-exist in a non-competitive environment." But that being the case, he asked Ramona how long she could delay the public pre-announcement regarding the John Doe recovery in Providence.

Ramona was puzzled by Bill's request. She wanted to know what would be accomplished by delaying the announcement. Bill got a little choked up when he explained he wanted their great Granddad to receive the public acknowledgement he so richly deserved. His life was snuffed-out as a result of a brutal attack at the hands of a group of red neck racists over 142 years ago. Bill indicated he believed by delaying the recovery announcement, until after the CMLB and MLB skirmish settled down, it would enable the recovery to take center stage.

Bill shifted gears when he directed his comments to Deborah and Ramona, asking whether they felt the Commissioner would use the recovery incident as a way to bolster his public persona. Deborah said, "If the Commissioner remains true to form, he will want to position MLB and himself as having the moral high ground. There would be no doubt he would relish the opportunity to muster up as many accolades as possible." Bill recommended the recovery announcement be delayed for at least three months to allow the firestorm between the two leagues to subside. At which time he would recommend Max from the Forensics department contact the Commissioner's office prior to the public release advising the Commissioner of their findings but not sharing with him the perpetrator's DNA direct linkage to his ancestor.

Deborah indicated that in her opinion the Commissioner would welcome the opportunity to showcase MLB by taking credit for moving forward the opening of a cold case of the ballplayer that mysteriously disappeared over 142 years ago. Bill said "So, if we all agree, that's our plan." They all nodded confirming their solidarity.

Chapter 29

The Beginning of the End

Three months later Bill and Bert were playing catch in a vacant back lot that was virtually in the shadows of MLB's 245 Park Avenue headquarters. Bert paced off 60 feet 6 inches, the exact distance Bill would be required to throw when he threw out the first pitch of the inaugural CMLB league game to be played at Cuba's Guillermo Moncada Stadium. Bill felt it was only fitting that the first game be played in the epicenter of the new CMLB league. That's not to say Raul Castro's insistence hadn't played a role in the final decision on the site selection for the first game between the Miami Pilots and Cuban Cienfuegos.

April 4, 2021 the launch date of the new CMLB would go down in history as the end of MLB's monopolistic practices. This date would also resonate in the annals of baseball history as the day the MLB Commissioner took it upon himself to launch a personal smear campaign against Bill and his entire organization, hoping to cause irreparable damage to the integrity of the new league. The Commissioner was determined to do whatever it took to blunt the news worthiness of the CMLB inaugural season. The Commissioner's actions hadn't come as a complete surprise. Bill and Deborah knew if the John Doe recovery story was leaked to the Commissioner's office prior to being released to the media, the Commissioner himself would want to get out front with the story, to control the narrative and position MLB in a positive proactive light. Of course, what the

Commissioner didn't count on was the full disclosure of what actually led to the search and eventual recovery of the first mixed race baseball player to play in a Major League Baseball game in 1879.

At 7:15 PM Bill made his way out to the pitcher's mound in the midst of 60,000 screaming baseball fans attending the first inaugural CMLB league game taking place at Cuba's Guillermo Mercado Stadium. As he prepared to hurl the ceremonial first pitch little did he know some 500 miles away, northeast, as the crow flies, the Commissioner of baseball was stepping up to the podium preparing to announce to the media the recovery of the remains of Brown University's mixed-race baseball player, Bill White, who in 1879 disappeared after being called out of the bleachers and signed to a one day contract to play for the home team, Major League Providence Grays of the National League.

Bill stepped on the mound and waved to the roaring crowd of 60,000 plus fans in attendance. He may have appeared to have it all together; in reality, his knees were knocking, and he could hardly catch his breath. His inner voice was telling him let's get it together. This is what you have dreamed about all your adult life. Bill took a deep breath, peered at home plate where Bert was positioned. Bill began his windup, mimicking the old school Satchel Page midnight rider pitch and hurled a perfect strike across home plate. The thunderous applause that followed was simply mind blowing. Bill's adrenaline was pumping so hard he felt as if he was floating on air as he made his way back to the dugout. The Cuban crowd rose to their feet to give Bill a heartfelt ovation, acknowledging not only the pitch but more importantly the national pride they were feeling now that their mother country was on a pedestal with the United States when it came to their beloved game of baseball. They perceived the launch of the new CMLB as a major step forward in the normalization of relations with their United States neighbors. The exhilaration Bill felt was numbing. As Bert high fived Bill for his pitching performance, he could see that Bill had tears welling up in his eyes. Bert assured Bill it was all good. Both Bill and Bert waved to the fans and headed down the steps into the visiting team's dugout.

As the Commissioner concluded his prepared remarks regarding the recovery of Bill White's remains, he extended his congratulations to the NYPD Forensics team for their exemplary efforts in solving the 142-year-old cold case. The Commissioner then opened the floor to answer questions from the fifty plus media staffers in attendance. The room was buzzing with curiosity to gain more insight into who was this Bill White; how did he just vanish. They were anxiously awaiting more details on what ignited the initial investigation into this particular cold case.

Reporters were told when posing their questions to position themselves at one of the three standing microphones positioned throughout the conference room. The first question came from the New York Times sports assignment editor, Phillip James. Phillip was directed to speak directly into the microphone when asking his question. Phillip directed his question to the Commissioner. What brought this particular cold case to the attention of the NYPD? The Commissioner thanked Phillip for his question and quickly redirected the question to the NYPD panel members, Ms. Ramona Green and Mr. Max Johnson.

Ms. Green was quick to point out that this particular cold case was still under investigation and as such, there were certain questions, she would not be able to address.   She did, however, go on to say her NYPD Forensic department received an anonymous phone call indicating the location of a certain clothing item that was believed to have been in the possession of the deceased when he was last seen leaving the then Providence Grays clubhouse on June 21, 1879. Ramona was interrupted by Phillip when he asked whether or not she was at liberty to say what the item in question was. Ms. Green responded by saying the police files indicated Mr. White left the clubhouse following the game with his uniform jersey and the actual lineup card for that night's game. She went on to say the actual line-up card was recovered and turned over to Mr. White's parents once the investigation was closed. When Ms. Green mentioned uniform jersey, you could see the Commissioners' demeanor starting to take a noticeable change. If one could read the Commissioner's mind you would realize he was starting to connect the dots. The vintage encased jersey in his office just happened to be a Providence Grays jersey that had been passed down over the years from his great great Grandpa. His pulse rate started to quicken as he pondered the remote likelihood a family member of his would have known the victim; even more worrisome would be if his ancestor had had something to do with the disappearance of Mr. White. His mental lapse was interrupted when Ms. Green indicated that her staff was successful in recovering two human DNA samples and one plant specimen. She was quick to point out they were confident they had matches for the two human specimens.

Ms. Green was interrupted by a follow-up question from Bill Smith of the Providence Gazette. "Ms. Green, are you prepared to share with us the names of those individuals associated with your DNA specimens?" Ms. Green reiterated that this was now an active investigation, and she was not at liberty to share names. She said that one of the DNA matches dates back to the late 1800's perhaps the DNA of one of the perpetrators who may have had a hand in the disappearance and possible murder of Mr. White. And the other Human DNA specimen, interestingly enough, appears to be a descendant of Mr. White. Almost in unison several reporters shouted out "When can we expect to have the names and the actual circumstances that led up to this discovery?" Ms. Green assured the group as soon as the investigation was completed her team would return to provide full details.

The Commissioner returned to the podium, but it was obvious he was stunned by what he had just heard. Unbeknownst to him, NYPD officers were in the process of serving Lynn, his administrative assistant, with a subpoena authorizing the confiscation of the vintage Providence Grays jersey from his office. They immediately removed the jersey from its plexiglas case and repositioned the now empty case back on the wall at its original location. They provided Lynn with a receipt for the item they removed and off they went. By this time, the Commissioner had concluded the press conference which turned out to be the most excruciating experience of his entire life.

As he began to make his way back to his office on the 6th floor, he came face to face with Ms. Green. He asked her what comes next and when could his office expect to receive an update from the NYPD. He hoped to gain her commitment to provide his office with the NYPD findings prior to releasing them to the general public. Ms. Green indicated this was a fluid investigation and she couldn't make any promises, but she would do all she could to make his office aware of any new developments as they occurred.

The Commissioner thanked her, said his goodbyes and made his way to his office. When he got off the elevator, he could see his administrative assistant at her desk with her face buried in her hands. As he approached her desk, peripheral vision enabled him to see into his office to the far right of Lynn's outer office. At that moment pure panic kicked in as he realized the plexiglas case that once housed his family's prized vintage Providence Grays jersey was now empty. Lynn gazed up as the Commissioner approached her office, her eyes swelled up with tears as she handed him the subpoena receipt she was given by the NYPD officers as they carried off the jersey.

Chapter 30

Say It Ain't So

Six months later Bill, Deborah, Ramona, Bert, Max and Molly were all settled in the front pew in New York's St. Patrick's Cathedral as Bill White's Providence Grays jersey draped casket lay in state. As guest Pastor Olin concluded his heartfelt eulogy you could sense a feeling of sorrow for a life of unbridled hope and promise that was not to be. One could only imagine incredible adulation Bill White experienced as he departed the clubhouse; only to have his hopes and aspirations extinguished by a group of racist bigots who viewed themselves as the privileged majority and him as being less than human.

As Bill sat next to Deborah with his arm draped around her shoulders, he couldn't help but reflect on his team's courageous accomplishments in starting a new league. Solving their ancestral discovery of Bill White. While at the same time, realizing the advent of social justice movements such as, "Me Too" and "Black Lives Matter," were a constant reminder, that as a society we still have work to do to instill a moral compass that simply judging people on their talents and not on the color of their skin, or their social economic status. He knew working to gain equality for all those whose dreams had yet to be realized, had to be the end game.

Less than two miles away, as the crow flies, the Commissioner is seen packing his personal effects into a 18x24 Bekins moving box as MLB's Chief of Security, Ian Robinson, patiently waited to unceremoniously escort the recently fired MLB Commissioner out of MLB's 245 Park avenue headquarters building. In an unprecedented move, the majority of small market team owners had voted to remove the Commissioner from office for his numerous missteps but none so egregious as his total miscalculation of the economic impact the new CMLB would have on MLB's revenue streams. The Commissioner's flawed attempts to crush the new CMLB ultimately led to his demise. The CMLB first full season overall performance strategically positioned The CMLB as a worthy adversary and an outright game changer going forward. Not only did the new league survive, it thrived in fan attendance, revenue generation, charitable contributions and player retention. To make things worse it had come to light that the Commissioner had in fact colluded with certain big market team owners in an effort to remove the luxury tax provision that ensures the survivability of small market teams while maintaining the competitive balance within the league.

The final nail in Jake's coffin occurred when certain owners mysteriously received a USB Flash drive that revealed the entire audio of the elevator episode when he exposed himself to Deborah. All these factors had sealed Jake's fate. The MLB owners were now keenly aware that the lack of leadership in the Commissioner's office had made them vulnerable to a worthy adversary that had shown they were here to stay.

As the funeral procession made its way outside St. Patrick's Cathedral on to the Avenue of the Americas, Deborah comforted Bill as they watched the draped casket being rolled into the Cadillac hearse. She whispered in his ear, "We did it." Bill smiled and said, "Yes, we did".

Two years later Bill and Deborah, now husband and wife arrive, at Bill's Dad's Brooklyn brownstone located in the Dumbo district. They rang the doorbell which started Molly barking. After three rings and no response, Bill, Jr. turned the doorknob and they entered the front foyer. They see Bill, Sr. (Dad) and Lil Rae Jr. fast asleep with Rae Jr. holding what appears to be a plastic whiffle bat, clutched in his little hand.

The End

POSTLOGUE
The Rest of the Story

The Jersey is a fact fictional adaptation of a true event. The story is of a mulatto college baseball player from Brown University participating in a Major League baseball game on June 21, 1879. William Edward White was a member of the Brown University 1879 National Collegiate Baseball Championship team. William was the son of prosperous Caucasian, Captain Andrew Jackson White and Captain White's mulatto slave mistress, known to history only as Aunt Hannah White. Captain White's will of 1877 indicate William Edward White and his two siblings, Anna Nora White and Sarah Adelaide White were children of his servant Hannah. He stipulated William and a sister "now at school in the North" be able to complete their education. William's cameo appearance was short lived as he was replaced by future Hall of Famer, Jim O'Rourke, in the next game. William departed Brown University following his junior year and migrated to the Chicago area where he started his career as a Draftsman. He passed in 1937 after falling on an icy sidewalk, breaking his hip and forearm and eventually dying from hypothermia on March 29, 1937 at the age of 76.

From all indications, while attending Brown University and during his move to the North, William appeared to be living as a white person. On both the 1900 and 1910 federal censuses William declared his race as White. W. Zachary Malinowski points out in his essay originally published in *Inventing Baseball: The 100 Greatest Games of the 19th Century,*

"By the retroactive application of genetic rules, William Edward White is the first known Black man to play major-league baseball. Within his society, however, he was not. He played baseball and lived his life as a white man. If White, who was also of White blood, said he was white and he was not challenged, he was white in his time and circumstances".

Bill McCurdy, Principal Writer, Editor, Publisher of the *Pecan Park Eagle* so eloquently stated:

"Racism is the human race cancer. And it needs to die. In all forms. As this man did, no one ever should have to pass for white, just to get a foot in the door. And that's why it's important to remember people like William Edward White, even if others suffered far more by comparison. No one among us should have to go through what he encountered to hide his true identity for the simple sake of avoiding someone else's need to **Hate.**"

William Edward White

(1860-1937)

First African-American

Major-League Baseball Player

By T.J. White

Introduction

The supposed, received 'facts' of history composing the socio-cultural, quasi-mythological narrative any given society largely comes to accept and believe, and by which it defines itself, are sometimes, as it turns out, dead-wrong. Several examples of this could be instanced, had we the time to explore them. Only one of them, however, concerns us now.

The late, great Jackie Robinson is justly celebrated for courageously breaking the color barrier for African-Americans in American baseball in 1947, playing for the Brooklyn Dodgers. But was he truly the first African-American ever to actually play major-league baseball? Recent research within the last decade has all but conclusively proven that he was not, in fact, the very first to play major-league baseball, even if there is no doubt that he is the most famous and justly-celebrated pioneering African-American player.

So just who was the first-ever African-American to play major-league, professional baseball?

His name was William Edward White, and he was from Georgia.

His story was first reported in a Wall Street Journal article of January the 30th, 2004, a story which was quickly repeated on the same day by ESPN. These articles were based primarily on research of Civil War historian Bruce Allardyce, genealogist Mark Arslan, and (mainly) Peter Morris, a researcher with the Society for American Baseball Research (SABR). Then, the story went cold for almost a decade (no further details emerging on the life of William Edward White).i

There is no doubt that William Edward White, an eighteen-year-old college student/athlete at the time, did in fact substitute in one major-league game in 1879. According to an April 22, 2013 article in Slate.com, the only real issue concerning whether or not baseball should officially recognize William Edward White as the first-ever "African-American" major-league baseball player, is "whether the sport should recognize a one-quarter black man who played one game as a substitute, and possibly did that without anyone knowing that he was black."ii

Herewith we will first present only the actual facts pertaining to William Edward White, as objectively as we know how; afterward, however, will follow a quite subjective commentary, based upon and extrapolating from those facts, which some may perhaps find unduly harsh or even unwarranted. This commentary is solely the writer's opinion, and no more.

The Facts, as Known or Believed

William Edward White was born in Milner, Pike (now Lamar) County, Georgia, in October, 1860.iii He was thus technically, at least, born into slavery. The fact that his mother was a mulatto made him (as mentioned) only one-quarter black (what would have been called back then a "quadroon"), though this percentage would have made him legally "black" in most states at that time.[iv]

He showed up as a nine-year-old "mulatto" with his "mulatto" mother Hannah, "black" grandmother Sarah, and two sisters (also "mulatto"), in the 1870 census of Milner, Pike County, Georgia.[v] This census was dated August 20th, 1870. (He has not yet been located in the 1860 census—and may not have even been born yet when his mother was enumerated.)

On June 13th, 1877, his father wrote out his (the father's) last will and testament, in Pike (now Lamar) County, Georgia. In this document, neither William Edward White nor his two sisters are actually referred to as "son" or "daughters," since they were one quarter African, former slaves, and also technically illegitimate. However, from the great care their father took to provide for them, including providing for their education, it appears plainly obvious that he tenderly loved (and defended) them, in a manner that only a natural or adoptive parent usually would. In this document, William and the elder of his two sisters ("Anna Nora White") are referred to as being "now at school in the North."[vi]

In the 1880 census, taken on June 12th, 1880, William Edward White was indeed listed as being "at school in the North." (He was also listed as being 'Caucasian'.) He was resident that year in Providence, Rhode Island, and was a student at Brown University, whose records do indeed list him as a student there, and as being born in Milner, Georgia, and a son of A.J. White.[vii]

Only one year previously, while still a student at Brown (a Baptist college known for taking in former slaves and free persons of color), William Edward White participated in the one and only major-league game which put him in the record books. The circumstances of this game, which took place on June 21st, 1879, were as follows: William Edward White, only eighteen years old at the time, and a member of his colleges ball club, filled in for ailing first baseman Joe Start, of the Major-League Providence Grays. White "got a hit, scored a run, fielded [twelve] plays flawlessly at first base—and never played in the majors again."[viii] He was replaced in the next game, we are told, by Hall of Famer "Orator Jim" O'Rourke.[ix] To this day it is unknown why he never again played in the majors. However, it is tempting to speculate (as some have done) that he may have been attempting to 'pass' as 'White' (Caucasian), may have been "found out," and may even have been threatened with loss of his position on his college team, if he continued to play major-league sports. This scenario, if true, would certainly handily account for why he never again played a major-league game.

Only one day after this historic game, William Edward White's participation therein was noticed in at least one major newspaper, The Chicago Tribune, which reported young White's participation as follows: "[First baseman Joe] Start having obtained leave of absence, White, first baseman of the Brown University nine, was substituted, and played the position with remarkable activity and skill for an amateur."[x]

Some five years before the 1880 census, both William Edward White and his sister Anna Nora White showed up as "students," both born in Georgia, in the Rhode Island State Census of 1875. William and his sister Anna were both listed as boarders at the "Friends [Quaker] Boarding School" in the City of Providence.[xi]

On Sunday, November 6th, 1988—long before he had ever heard of William Edward White as a baseball player at Brown University (still less as a record-setter), this writer travelled to the Baptist Church in Milner, Georgia, for purposes of researching William Edward White's father. While there, he met and interviewed a Mrs. Sallie Woodall Domingos (1907-2002), former church historian of the congregation there, and one of the two people responsible for erecting the tombstone in the church cemetery for William White's father (who had been a benefactor to the church many years earlier). Mrs. Domingos, who, in 1988, was already elderly, and along with one elderly gentleman named Jack Morgan, also a member of the congregation, told this writer that they personally remembered seeing William Edward White's mother Hannah sitting in the back of the church during worship services. They were both very young at the time, of course. These events probably took place in the late Nineteen-Twenties, or early Nineteen-Thirties. Mrs. Domingos, who told this writer several other interesting anecdotes about William Edward White's parents and family, confirmed for this writer that William and his two sisters were indeed known, in the small, tight-knit Milner community, to have been illegitimate children of Capt. A.J. White (as he was known at Milner Baptist Church), and his mulatto former slave mistress, "Aunt" Hannah White (as she was known to the congregation). Mrs. Domingos further elaborated that William and his two sisters "went up North," and—except for the youngest sibling, a sister—never once returned to visit either of their parents. "They were trying to pass as 'White'," said Mrs. Domingos, of the three children, "and were never heard from again."[xii] This story, while certainly anecdotal, does nonetheless have the ring of veracity, and can serve as supporting evidence of the already-suspected guess as to the reason for William Edward White's sudden retirement from major-league sports, after having played only one game. Suddenly, the pieces seem to have fallen into place.

Lending still further support to our theory that William Edward White, who—according to Mrs. Domingos of Milner, Georgia (who personally knew his mother), was attempting to "pass" as 'White' while at school in Providence—was somehow "found out" as being 'Black', is the other known fact that he mysteriously left Brown University—whence his very wealthy father had sent him to obtain all the advantages of a premier education—sometime after 1880, without taking his degree. Other than sheer disinterest, why else would any young mixed-race person whose socio-economic standing and future, always so precarious, depended absolutely on obtaining a decent education, actually quit his college studies, freely paid for by his father, and leave without a degree? Absent the "found out" theory, these circumstances would boggle the mind.

The 1890 Federal Census, of course, no longer exists, so we have no easy way of knowing just where William Edward White was living about that time. However, we do have record of his marriage, in Chicago, Cook County, Illinois, on the 20th of April, 1893, so he probably arrived in Chicago not many years prior to his marriage. His wife, who was Caucasian, was named Harriet B. "Hattie" Hill, and was nineteen at the time of her marriage (thus born circa 1874). Her husband listed his name as "Will" E. White.[xiii]

The 1900 Census of Chicago (June 8th, 1900) again lists "William E. White," as a white male, with his new wife "Hattie"; he was born in October, 1860 in "Rhode Island" instead of Georgia (thus enabling us to tie him to his former residence and ever-so-brief sports profession), and his occupation in 1900 was "bookkeeper." His wife Hattie's birthplace was listed as Elgin, Cook County, Illinois, and her date of birth as September 1872. With them were two female children, Gladys, born in Illinois in October, 1894, and Vera, born also in Illinois in April, 1897. William incorrectly said that both of his parents were also born in "Rhode Island."[xiv]

William Edward White was clearly telling the census-takers (at the very least), up to this point, that he was "Caucasian," because the 1910 Census of Chicago, Cook County, Illinois, again lists "Will E. White," as a white male, aged forty-nine (born circa 1860-1861), born in "Rhode Island," with parents born in "Virginia" (there is some truth to this, for his father's ancestors did come from that state). With him again was his wife Hattie B., aged thirty-seven, born in Illinois, and the two children aforementioned (Gladys H. aged fifteen, and Vera A., aged 12, both white females), but this time there was an additional third child, another daughter named J. Bernice White, a white female, aged 2. Hattie reported again, as she had in 1900, that her father had been born in England, and her mother in New York. This census was dated April 25th, 1910, and William listed his occupation as a draftsman in the "car works" industry. As in 1900, he was again renting his house in 1910.[xv]

We know very little about William Edward White's daughters, with the partial exception of his eldest, for whom a few additional records have been located. She was Gladys H. White, and was born in Chicago on October 29th, 1894. She married a white man named Albert H. Bierma (seemingly of Dutch origin), and died on August 6th, 1926, again in Chicago, after a tragically-short life. She lies buried in the massive Forest Home Cemetery in Cook County.xvi A search of the online records for that cemetery at Find-a-Grave.com failed to locate any records of any other members of her family (even her husband, who may have remarried). Similarly, neither of William Edward White's sisters has successfully been traced, at this point in time. The 1880 Census of Chicago shows a Samuel Hill, aged forty-six, who was born in England, with a wife named Mary J., aged twenty-nine, who was born in Illinois. These people may have been the parents of William's wife Hattie. It is entirely possible that none of William's descendants (assuming he has living descendants today) know that their ancestor was one-quarter Black.

By the time of the 1920 Census, William Edward White and his wife Hattie and their daughters had, for whatever unknown reason, parted company: he may have been the man listed as William White, aged sixty, as a "widowed" black male, born in Georgia (and with parents both born in Georgia), residing alone in the City of Harvey, Cook County, Illinois, a place which is clearly among the suburbs on Chicago's "Black" south side. This William White was enumerated on January 29th, 1920, and listed his occupation as contracting out his labor.xvii But our William Edward White's wife Hattie was in fact very much alive in 1920: on the 6th of January, 1920, she and her three daughters were enumerated in Ward 35 of the City of Chicago, renting a house at 4117 W. Harrison Street. Hattie listed herself as still being "married," though with no trace of her husband. Hattie again listed her father as having been born in England, and her mother in New York. The three daughters claimed their father to have been born in "Rhode Island." The two older daughters, Gladys and Vera, were both listed as bank cashiers, and their mother and youngest sister with no occupation.xviii We do not know what had become of their father William, nor why he was not enumerated with his family that year (nor again in the following 1930 census), and can only speculate as to the possible reasons. Certainly, two possibilities immediately suggest themselves to us: William Edward White could have felt a twinge of conscience, and have decided to confess his bi-racial status to his wife and daughters (though in the age of 'Jim Crow' Segregation, this is probably highly unlikely); conversely, he could have again been "exposed" as being "Black" instead of "White," and could have either been disowned by his wife or children, or felt duty-bound to leave them. Unfortunately, we may very well never know the real cause or causes of this separation. Regardless of the reason, though, it seems clear that he was no longer living with his wife and family, at some point after 1910, and before 1920.

By the time of the 1930 Census, taken on April 19th, 1930, his eldest daughter was already dead, and thus no longer with the family. Enumerated again without their father and husband were Vera A. White, a white female aged thirty-two, as the head of household, together with her "widowed" mother Hattie B., a white female aged fifty-six, and sister Bernice, a white female aged twenty-two. All were born in Illinois. Hattie again listed her father's birthplace as "England," and that of her mother as "New York." Vera and her sister Bernice again claimed their father's birthplace as "Rhode Island." Also listed in the household was a Lucille M. Ryan, a white female aged nineteen, who was described as a daughter of Vera A. White. This Lucille gave her birthplace as "New York," and that of her missing father—presumably named "Ryan," as the "Irish Free State." The members of this household were renting rooms in an apartment house described as being at N. Parkside and Washington Blvd., in Block 538 of Ward 37 of the City of Chicago. Vera listed her occupation as "private secretary" for a bank; her sister Bernice gave hers as "General Office Work"; their mother as "none," and their daughter/niece Lucille as "clerical work" in a "dress shop."[xix]

A man named "William White" was listed as having died in Chicago, Cook County, Illinois, on the 29th of March, 1937. This William White's wife was listed as "Hattie White," so this would certainly seem to be our man, though final proof is lacking.[xx] No burial location was given in this record, alas. Again, why husband and wife would apparently be listed together at the time of his death in 1937, but not in the earlier 1920 or 1930 censuses, is a real mystery, one that may well never be solved.

Parentage and Ancestry

As alluded to above, the father of our William Edward White was Captain Andrew Jackson "A.J." "Jack" White, born in Elbert County, Georgia on 25 April, 1815, a son of Reuben White and his wife Elizabeth "Betsy" Heard. Captain A.J. White, a wealthy land speculator, sometime captain of the "Holloway Grays," Company E, 3rd Georgia Battalion, C.S.A., and also later the powerful president of the Central of Georgia Railroad, died in Milner, Georgia, on 12 December, 1888. He was a co-founder of the Baptist church in Milner, Georgia, his adopted hometown (and in whose cemetery he lies buried). The town of Whitesburg, in Carroll County, Georgia, presently home of the celebrated "BanningMills" resort, was named in his honor, because of his heavy speculative land holdings in the area at the time the town was organized.[xxi]

Captain A.J. White had an illustrious Colonial Virginia ancestry, a family which included the diarist Jeremiah White Sr. (1695-1776) (his great-grandfather). U.S. President George Washington was his second cousin, three times removed. The present Queen of England is his fifth cousin, five times removed. Another distant living cousin through this same paternal ancestor, Jeremiah White Sr., albeit in a female line, is the famous contemporary film actress Uma Thurman, whose paternal great-grandmother Huella Bedford Thurman (born 1885) was herself a great-granddaughter of Sarah S. White McGehee (1799-1838), of Elbert and Oglethorpe Counties, Georgia, herself a great-granddaughter of Jeremiah White Jr. (1728-1788), a son of the aforementioned Jeremiah Sr. Actress Uma Thurman is thus a third cousin, five times removed, to Captain A.J. White (and six times removed, to William Edward White, his son the baseball player). Through this same enviable paternal ancestry, moreover, Captain A.J. White and his son William Edward White descend from generation after generation of English and European kings and emperors, including Charlemagne, and are related to a significant percentage of all Americans generally.[xxii]

William Edward White's mulatto mother Hannah was listed in the 1870 and 1880 censuses as having been born in Washington, D.C.

(Her fully 'Black' mother Sarah was born in Maryland circa 1820, according to the 1870 census.) The fact that Hannah White was born in Washington D.C. means that she may very likely have been born as a free person of color. But then she (apparently) willingly followed her lover, Captain A.J. White into certain slavery in Georgia, and bore him three slave children there! Other than assuming either that she was taken into slavery as a child, before she could have voiced her objections, or that she was simply in such terrible debt that she had no other choice but to relocate into a slave state, there is really only one reasonable explanation for such an extraordinary action: she must have been deeply in love with her man. In the 1870 census, she was listed as living separately from him, but by the time of the 1880 census, they had abandoned most of the pretense, and were living together, as a couple, but otherwise alone. (Her husband had purchased his home in Milner in the interim, in the year 1872.) They told the census-taker in 1880 (apparently for propriety's sake) that she was his "servant." It is a real shame that we know so little about the origins of her slave status, and the truth of her relationship to Captain A.J. White, because hers may have been one of the truly great and tragic love stories of our Western Culture, if only we were able to document it.

In the 1900 Federal Census of Pike County, taken on the 1st day of June of that year, Hannah White, "black," aged sixty, and born in April, 1840, was listed as a "Servant" in the household of a Marian F. Head, a widowed white female aged seventy-one (born in Georgia in January, 1829). Hannah thus seems to have found gainful employment of a sort after the 1888 death of her partner, Captain A.J. White.[xxiii]

In the 1910 Federal Census, the only likely apparent candidate to be this same Hannah White is a sixty-five year old "widowed" mulatto woman by that name, resident at 85 Harrell Street, in the old Fourth Ward of Atlanta, Fulton County, Georgia. This person was shown as having been born in "Maryland," which certainly fits with what we already know of William Edward White's mother Hannah. With this Hannah White in Atlanta in 1910 was a thirty-eight year old married mulatto "niece" named Annie L. [White?], who was born in Georgia.[xxiv]

Hannah White, mother of William Edward White, has thus far escaped easy identification in the 1920 Federal Census.

She did appear, however, in the 1930 Federal Census (April 3rd, 1930), in Milner, Lamar County, Georgia, as a "black" "widowed" female, living alone, aged 80 (thus born circa 1850), born in the "District of Columbia," with parents given as having been born in "Virginia."[xxv]

Our Hannah White apparently died in Lamar (formerly Pike) County, Georgia, on January 20th, 1931.[xxvi]

The last mention of Hannah White which we possess comes again from the aforementioned Mrs. Domingos, who recalled "Aunt Hannah" White as a small, wizened light-skinned (and still beautiful) old African-American woman who would always sit on the back pew in the Baptist Church of Milner, and who would faithfully and lovingly tend the grave of her "Captain White," keeping its white 'paling' fence in good repair, and fresh flowers regularly placed on his grave, until the day she died. Mrs. Domingos said that "Aunt Hannah," out of the respect which the congregation had for her late 'husband' Captain A.J. White, was always welcomed in this ostensibly 'White' congregation. Sadly, though, when asked about the burial location of 'Aunt Hannah' White, Mrs. Domingos reported that the Baptist Church membership would not stand for allowing Hannah to be buried next to her beloved Captain White, in a 'White' church cemetery, but instead relegated her to the town's Negro burying ground, where she was unceremoniously laid to rest in an unmarked grave. Sadly, Hannah's burial place remains unknown and unmemorialized to this day.[xxvii]

Sic transit gloria mundi ...

Epilogue: The 'Mark of Cain':

A Few Brief Observations on Racism, Stigmatization, and Dehumanization

The evidence concerning the life of William Edward White (perhaps because of his own intention) is mostly shadowy and often inconclusive. Yet the overall appearance and tenor clearly suggests that he may have lost, surrendered, or been deprived of, nearly every aspect of 'normal' life—education, career, residence, and even his family. We may never know if we are correct in making such a blanket assumption about him; however, in the following commentary, for the sake of discussion, this writer will proceed as if this was indeed the case (all the while freely admitting and cautioning that it may not have been). Whether or not it was true concerning William Edward White, it certainly was true regarding hundreds, if not thousands, of his contemporaries, and this fact may perhaps help justify this writer's coming tone and verbage. Moreover, it is this writer's considered opinion that such words as will follow need to be said, even if they may not apply to Mr. White.

William Edward White, to this writer at least, seems very much to have been a proverbial 'Man Without a Country'—in a manner much reminiscent of the protagonist of Conrad Richter's profound 1953 tale of alienation and exile, The Light in the Forest, or the protagonist of Jerzy Kosinski's equally-profound (and disturbing) 1965 novel, The Painted Bird—a perpetual 'outsider', forever caught between two opposing worlds, and never wholly at home or welcome in either. Philosophers Friedrich Nietzsche and Colin Wilson, too, each in his own distinctive way, discussed and sympathized with those outcast socio-cultural "Outsiders" who are forced to wear the "pallid mark of the Chandala" on their foreheads, forever set apart from their fellow-humans as 'different' or 'nferior'.[xxviii]

Because he evidently left no written record of his thoughts and emotions, despite having been an educated man, we can only make blind, guessing stabs at what William Edward White must have felt throughout his life, he who, from all available evidence, may have lost or given up his place at University, his place on the Brown University ball team, his very good chance at a major-league baseball career, and—last, but certainly not least—his very family: his wife and children—all apparently because of his ancestry and the color of his skin. It is scarcely an exaggeration to say that not since Old Testament Job, has one man apparently lost so much, within a single lifetime. Although we can only guess at how all these profound losses must have affected him (if we are correct in assigning them to him), something of the probable emotion involved was poignantly captured in this magnificent, though heart-rending, poem of his contemporary, Paul Laurence Dunbar (1872-1906):

We wear the mask

We wear the mask that grins and lies,
It hides our cheeks and shades our eyes—
This debt we pay to human guile;
With torn and bleeding hearts we smile,
And mouth with myriad subtleties.
Why should the world be over-wise,
In counting all our tears and sighs?

Nay, let them only see us, while
We wear the mask.
We smile, but, O great Christ, our cries
To thee from tortured souls arise.
We sing, but oh the clay is vile
Beneath our feet, and long the mile;
But let the world dream otherwise,
We wear the mask![xxix]

We can only guess at the kind of athlete, man, husband, and father William Edward White could have been, had his society merely allowed him to simply exist, on his own God-created terms. And, at this point, we will never know. We did, however, glimpse his potential as athlete, for one brief, ever-so-fleeting moment, on the fields of glory, and William Edward White's qualities shone then resplendently indeed, for all the world to witness. And we are simply stunned by what we saw, and then as quickly lost forever.

There are truly many decent and humane people living today, who are not racist or xenophobic, and who are also wonderfully compassionate and selflessly helpful toward their suffering fellow men. This writer personally knows several such people. Sadly, though, such people are in the minority. Also in a minority of their own are the despicable persons who are blatantly, irredeemably racist, xenophobic, inhumane, and intentionally cruel toward their otherwise innocent, but different, fellow humans—persons who seemingly delight in adding to the discomfort and sufferings of others whose only 'offense' was to have been born unique and different. This, of course, is most regrettable, though it is undeniably a fact.

Even worse are those racist and xenophobic people who cloak their virulent hatred in a 'hardshell', unforgiving version of the Christian religion, thus making a mockery of the founder of that faith, who accepted and loved everyone, regardless of differences. It was Gandhi who once famously said, in effect, that he greatly admired 'Jesus Christ,' and his doctrines, but could not himself consider becoming a 'Christian' because of the deplorable behavior of so many people who call themselves "Christians." What follows, therefore, will be purposely directed alone against those specific types of despicable human beings—those who maliciously and subversively cloak their venom in the dress of the beautiful, admirable religion of the 'Prince of Peace,' and the following paragraphs will intentionally use a 'Biblical' tone and language which will be readily comprehensible to them. Like Lincoln in his justly-famous speeches during the American Civil War, any latter-day 'prophet' calling a fundamentalist-minded body of people to 'repentance' would be well-advised (this writer believes) to do so in a language which the objects of his righteous wrath can well comprehend.

Of course, the vast majority of persons making up our present society probably fall well within the middle of the two widely opposing extremes outlined here, and it is to them that the oft-quoted phrase may sometimes apply: "All that is necessary for evil to triumph is for good men to do nothing." To the extent to which otherwise good, decent people "do nothing" with regard to racism, xenophobia, and persecution of unwanted minorities, they will therefore share somewhat in the following condemnation.

So, with sincere apologies to those readers of this essay who do not deserve to hear such harsh and 'Biblical' language as will follow (or who are not "Christian"), this writer will proceed:

What kind of society treats noble, upright, reasoning, moral, thinking, feeling, suffering human beings—the very "image of God"--as if they were rude, unkempt beasts of the field (or worse)? How can any society claim to be moral, or "right with God," which treats any of its members as second-class citizens (for any reason)? These difficult and thorny questions must still give us serious pause, even today, and our society, collectively, has yet to escape the burden of guilt for these crimes, because so much of our society continues to commit them against unwanted, despised, and feared minorities—yes, even today. We are clearly not yet out of the Wilderness, nor capable of resting securely in the Promised Land of God's favor and just blessing. Those who have not yet learned to overcome fear, hatred, racism, and xenophobia, deserve instead His severe upbraiding, and blighting curse. On behalf of all who continue to fall short in this regard, we should fervently pray God's mercies and forgiveness upon us, for our many individual and collective sins and crimes against our fellow-beings, who never did deserve such callous, calculated, cruel, and inhuman treatment at our hands (even if some of us, in our delusional thinking, may have once upon a time thought that they "deserved" such treatment).

And of course, the saddest and most tragic fact of all is that, even today, some people—apparently far too comfortable with their own sadistic and masochistic impulses toward domination and humiliation of others—do still smugly and self-righteously think that certain hapless classes of persons somehow "deserve" such inhuman and brutal treatment. It is this very troglodyte, delusional lie, a lie so horribly ugly and vicious, that it is loathsome and repugnant even to taste its name in one's mouth, which must be strenuously, vociferously, and perpetually spewed out and resisted at every possible turn, if we are not once again to see it inevitably lead--human nature unfortunately being what it is--to still greater jack-booted, Fascist-style official persecutions and genocides. Negative, harmful, or destructive human impulses must be resisted, and restrained, from the very moment they rear their ugly heads. And it all starts with proper education (though not mere "indoctrination"). An uninformed and apathetic populace, as has so often before been said, will only ignorantly repeat past mistakes.

It goes without saying that few of us can even begin to imagine what it must be like to have to try to live one's life in the shadows, constantly "on the run," never fully participating in the rich bounty life can and should afford, ashamed of and loathing one's very existence, and constantly in a state of debilitating fear of being "found out," of having one's whole life forever ruined, in the literal "blink of an eye." Some people within living memory, however, know this experience: gays and lesbians, for example, who lived through America's conformity-loving, xenophobic "McCarthy Era" of the Nineteen-Fifties, will know. Certain others, too, unfortunately placed in similar situations, will know. This is not in any way to diminish the awful fact that so many innocent people have lost their lives to mob violence; nonetheless, it almost does not matter at all whether or not 'Jim Crow'-style vigilante physical violence or even death are ever invoked, for--as awful and unconscionable as vigilante murders or beatings are--society can only, after all, murder the physical body but once. Thereafter, the Soul is at well-deserved peace. The mental and emotional anguish, torture, and terror, however, are, if anything, far worse, and more perniciously evil, because they are more insidious, and far more long-lasting. Most people, almost needless to say, cannot even begin to imagine the kind of mercilessly unending torture of soul being forced to live like this involves, and thus usually wrongly think the physical torture to be the worse of the two.

But let us at least, and at long last, try to remedy this much: let us humbly restore to William Edward White, in his lifetime hated, shunned, feared, ostracized, and practically exiled, and apparently deprived at every turn of every single blessing and opportunity (save life only), which you and I take so much for granted, some small measure of the credit and human dignity denied him during his life. He deserves no less, and (clearly) so much more.

This brief article is an attempt to do just that.

Decani ubi saeva indignatio

cor ulterius lacerare nequit ...

Requiescas in Pace, frater meus.

---

i Wall Street Journal (online), "Mystery of Baseball: Was William White Game's First Black?", http://online.wsj.com/article/0,,SB10

7541676333815810,00.html , ESPN.com (online), "Was William Edward White really first?", http://espn.go.com/espn/print?id=1723322&type=story , Wikipedia, "William Edward White," http://en.wikipedia.org/wiki/William_Edward_White .

ii Slate.com (online),

http://www.slate.com/articles/sports/sports_nut/2013/04/william_edward_white_was_a_little-known_19th-century_man_the_first

_black_player_in_major-league_history?

iii 1870 United States Federal Census, Pike County, Georgia, page 241 (Ancestry.com); 1880 United States

Federal Census, Providence, Rhode Island, Supervisor's District 1,

Enumeration District 17, page 34

(Ibid.); 1900 United States Federal Census, Chicago, Cook County, Illinois, Supervisor's District 1,

Enumeration District 1092, sheet 13 (which incorrectly lists his birthplace as "Rhode Island.") (Ibid.);

"Was William Edward White really first?"by the Associated Press, via ESPN.com, Friday, January 30,

2004, retrieved from http://espn.go.com/espn/ print?id=1723322&type=story . (This article mentions the

fact that records at Brown University say that student William Edward White was a son of A.J. White of

Milner, Georgia.)

iv Slate.com, Ibid.

v 1870 United States Federal Census, Pike County, Georgia, page 241.

vi 1880 United States Federal Census, Providence, Rhode Island, Supervisor's District 1, Enumeration

District 17, page 34 (Ancestry.com); Pike County, Georgia Will Book D (1876-1914), pp. 148-152. (Will of

Andrew J. White, #716.) On microfilm at the Georgia State Archives, Morrow, Georgia.

vii Slate.com, Ibid.; Wikipedia, Ibid.

viii Slate.com, Ibid.

ix Wikipedia, Ibid.

x The Chicago Tribune, Sunday, June 22, 1879, page 7 (Fold3.com)

xi Rhode Island State Censuses, 1865-1935 (1875) (Ancestry.com)

xii Author interview with Mrs. Sally Woodall Domingos, Milner,

Georgia, Sunday, November 6th, 1988

(unpublished notes).

xiii "Cook County, Illinois, Marriages Index, 1871-1920" (Ancestry. com)

xiv 1900 United States Federal Census, Chicago, Cook County, Illinois, Supervisor's District 1,

Enumeration District 1092, sheet 13 (Ancestry.com)

xv 1910 United States Federal Census, Supervisor's District 1, Enumeration District 672, sheet 10A

(Ancestry.com)

xvi "Illinois, Deaths and Stillbirths, 1916-1947" (FamilySearch.org)

xvii 1920 United States Federal Census, Supervisor's District 2, Enumeration District 215, sheet 22B

(Ancestry.com)

xviii 1920 United States Federal Census, Supervisor's District 1, Enumeration District 2247, sheet 4A

(Ancestry.com)

xix 1930 United States Federal Census, Supervisor's District 4, Enumeration District 16-1302, sheet 29A

(Ancestry.com)

xx "Illinois, Deaths and Stillbirths, 1916-1947" (FamilySearch.org)

xxi Georgia's Last Frontier: the Development of Carroll County, by James C. Bonner, pages 96-97

(http://dlg.galileo.usg.edu/meta/html/dlg/ugapressbks/meta_dlg_ugapressbks_ugp9780820335254.html?Welcome).

xxii Personal research of the author.

xxiii 1900 United States Federal Census, Milner, Pike County, Georgia, Supervisor's District 6, Enumeration

District 82, Sheet Number 1.

xxiv 1910 United States Federal Census, Milner, Pike County, Georgia, Supervisor's District 5, Enumeration

District 72, Sheet Number 33B.

xxv 1930 United States Federal Census, Milner, Lamar County, Georgia, Supervisor's District 7,

Enumeration District 86-7, Sheet Number 2B

xxvi "Georgia Deaths, 1919-1998" (Ancestry.com)

xxvii Author interview, op. cit.

xxviii The Portable Nietzsche (Google Books) (inter alia), page 550

(http://books.google.com/books?id=blfwSlxhjvAC&pg=PA550&lpg=PA550&dq=pallid+mark+of+the+chandala&source=bl&ots=kqVqi8NrJN&sig= ttZa5hsIypxGB4YzKAEAQ2AlBNA&hl=en&sa=X&ei=USMz UpaVFIbE9gTr4GIDA&ved=0CEoQ6AEwBA#v=onepage&q=pallid%20mark%20of%20the%20chandala&f=false).

xxix The Poetry Foundation.org, http://www.poetryfoundation.org/poem/173467

xxx Forty percent of living American whites have zero black friends, per a 2013 Reuters poll (http://www.reuters.com/article/2013/08/08/us-usa-poll-race-idUSBRE97704320130808). Also, 2013 Presidential Medal of Freedom recipient Bayard Rustin, who organized the famous 1963 "March on Washington" which culminated in Dr. King's justly-famous "I Have a Dream Speech," was also forced to register as a 'sexual offender,' in part (at least) because of his open homosexuality. (California Reform Sex Offender Laws website, http://californiarsol.org/2013/09/registrant-recipient-of-presidential-medal-offreedom/). At least one recent court case has held these registration requirements to be unduly harsh and punitive, and in violation of the Ex Post Facto Clause of the U.S. Constitution (http://cjonline.com/sites/default/files/offenderDecision.pdf).

William E. White

Articles & Photos

William White. 1st Base
PROVIDENCE PARK BALL CLUB

Mystery of Baseball: Was William White Game's First Black?

* * *

He Played a Big League Game In 1879—Then Vanished; Mr. Morris Picks Up Trail

By Stefan Fatsis

ZEBULON, Ga.—For years, William Edward White was just an obscure 19th-century big-league baseball player.

The biographical record for Mr. White, who played in only one game, in 1879, lacked a date of birth, a date of death and a place of death. Then a search for such details of his life yielded an astonishing question: Was William Edward White a black man? If so, he would be the first known black player in major-league history.

Most people think Jackie Robinson became the first African-American in the big leagues when he broke baseball's color line in 1947 with the Brooklyn Dodgers. But students of the sport know that technically that isn't true. While Mr. Robinson ushered in a new era in modern sports history, Moses Fleetwood Walker, a black man, played 42 games for the Toledo Blue Stockings of the American Association in 1884, and his brother, Weldy, played a few games for the same team that season. Historians say the major leagues date to 1871, when the National Association was formed.

For a small group of amateur historians who hunt down missing pieces in the lives of long-forgotten players, discovering a new "first" black major leaguer would be an important and newsworthy event. The researchers, who are members of the biographical committee of the Society for American Baseball Research, or SABR, are otherwise engaged in a broader, less dramatic effort: compiling complete biographical data—especially full names and birth and death records—for all 16,002 men who have played in the majors. With the help of online databases such as census and cemetery listings, baseball sleuths have whittled the number of missing death records down to just 344, half as

Please Turn to Page A6, Column 1

Have Sleuths Discovered New 'First' in Baseball?

Continued From First Page

many as two decades ago.

Some of the missing will probably never be found, like the fellow named Smith who may have come out of the stands to play in a game in 1888. But the search has unearthed some fascinating stories, such as that of Walter Walker, who appeared in one game in 1884. A researcher found that Mr. Walker later spent 30 years in an insane asylum. "To me, everybody that played in the major leagues is important," says Bill Carle, chairman of the SABR biographical committee, who keeps a master list of incomplete records. "I don't like seeing these holes."

A handful of SABR researchers had looked into William Edward White's past. They knew, for example, that as a student he played first base for Brown University in Providence, R.I. They also knew that on June 21, 1879, he filled in for the big-league Providence Greys of the National League. He got a hit, scored a run and fielded 12 plays without error.

The Chicago Tribune reported the next day that Mr. White "played the position with remarkable activity and skill for an amateur." But even though the Greys' regular first baseman was out for a month with a broken finger, Mr. White never returned to the Enemy.

Records from Brown stated that Mr. White was born in 1860 in Milner, Ga.; that the son of A.J. White and left school in 1890 without graduating. The 1890 census placed him in Providence. After that, nothing. "The fact is that it's a very common name," says Richard Malatzky, a SABR sleuth who worked on Mr. White.

The trail stayed cold until Peter Morris, a prolific SABR biographical researcher, contacted fellow baseball gum-

Hennes & Mauritz AB

Hennes & Mauritz AB posted a 1% drop in fourth-quarter net profit, but the retailer said sales in December, the first month of its first quarter, grew 11%. H&M, which sells fashionable clothes at low prices at 941 stores in 14 countries, said net profit in the fourth quarter ended Nov. 30 fell to 2.27 billion kronor ($293.5 million) from 2.29 billion kronor. The Swedish company blamed the fall in earnings on unfavorable currency effects and weak sales from its winter collection of knitwear, coats and jackets, but said that lower costs limited the decline. Sales edged up 2.2% to 16.35 billion kronor, indicating a decline in sales at stores open more than a year.

shoe and Civil War historian Bruce Allardice. Mr. Allardice had cracked the case of two men named Charles Householder—who played at the same time in the 1880s. Mr. Morris told him about William White. A few weeks later, Mr. Allardice e-mailed back.

"Is it possible this guy is black?" he asked.

Searching the 1880 census, Mr. Allardice found that the only A.J. White in Milner, Ga., was Andrew J. White. Mr. White, 45 years old, listed no wife or children. But his household included a 16-year-old mulatto woman named Hannah White.

Mr. Allardice got in touch with Mark Aubun, a genealogist of the White family. Mr. Aubun said 1860 census records showed A.J. White owning 70 slaves. Both researchers found Hannah White on the 1870 census. She was living with her mother and three children. One of them was a 5-year-old mulatto boy named William White.

Ten years later, William White would have been of college age. Brown at the time was affiliated with the Baptist church, and A.J. White built the Baptist church in Milner. Newspapers described him as a well-to-do merchant and railroad president, so he would have had the means to send a mixed-race child north to be educated. "All of this is just fitting together perfectly," Mr. Allardice says.

Mr. Morris remembered that a SABR colleague, John Husman, had a great-grandfather who played for Brown in the 19th century. Mr. Husman had a photo of the 1879 team. It shows William White standing behind the manager. His skin appears to be darker than that of his peers.

For Mr. Morris, the picture prompted an interesting conjecture. Mr. White was one-quarter black, which made him legally black under most state laws. Brown admitted black students, but Mr. White identified himself as white on the 1880 census. Did he pay only one big-league game because his racial background was discovered?

Until the late 1880s, it wasn't unusual for blacks and whites to play together in semipro and minor leagues in the North. But tensions existed, and blacks gradually were drummed out of white teams, says David Zang, the author of a biography of Fleetwood Walker.

Earlier this month, Mr. Morris, 41, took a week off from his job as a researcher for a Michigan public-health interest group and drove the 1,000 miles from his home to Georgia. His aim: To definitively link William Edward White to A.J. White and to find out what happened to the ballplayer after 1890.

First stop was the University of Georgia, in Athens. In the main library, Mr. Morris scoured microfilm, spotting obitu-

aries of A.J. White but little else. At the public library in Macon the next day, Mr. Morris found A.J. White in a book on Confederate soldiers, in a local railroad history and in newspapers. Mr. White receiving "One negro man" in a court ruling; attending Whig Party meetings; offering and during a yellow-fever epidemic. Interesting, but, Mr. Morris said, "it doesn't get us any closer to his son."

A librarian directed Mr. Morris to the courthouse in Zebulon, an hour away, which held probate records for Milner, where A.J. White died. The next morning, a clerk pulled down two thick plastic binders containing wills recorded in Pike County, Ga., from 1867 to 1946, on page 18 of the first volume. Mr. Morris found Mr. White's will, dated 1877.

"Item Fourth," Mr. Morris read, "All the balance of my Estate, both Real and Personal of Every Kind and description ... I do hereby ... bequeath unto William Edward White, Anna Nora White, and Sarah Adelaide White, the children of my servant Hannah."

"There's your proof," Mr. Morris said quietly.

The mention of William Edward White confirmed his full name and the link to A.J. White. A bonus: "Item Eighth" stipulated that William and a sister "now at School in the North" be able to complete their education.

That A.J. didn't identify William as his son, which was how he was listed at Brown, wasn't surprising in the South after the Civil War. That he left all of his money and property to a "servant" and her children was unusual, historians say, and probable confirmation of a deeper relationship. "It's nice to find that people behave better than you expect," Mr. Morris said over hash across from the courthouse.

From Zebulon, Mr. Morris drove to Milner. On a cold and dustry afternoon, he wandered among tombstones dating to the 1800s. Finally, Mr. Morris walked over a modern granite marker: "Capt. A.J. White, Benefactor of Milner Baptist Church." He was buried alone.

Peter Morris

The 1879 Brown University baseball team, William Edward White is seated directly behind the team manager, who is dressed in black.

William Edward White

William Edward White (October 1860 – March 29, 1937) was a 19th-century American baseball player. He played as a substitute in one professional baseball game for the Providence Grays of the National League, on June 21, 1879.[1] Work by the Society for American Baseball Research (SABR) suggests that he may have been the first African-American to play major league baseball, predating the longer careers of Moses Fleetwood Walker and his brother Weldy Walker by five years; and Jackie Robinson by 68 years.[2][3][4][5][6]

William Edward White	

White photographed as a member of the 1879 Brown University baseball team	
First baseman	
Born: October 1860 Milner, Georgia	
Died: March 29, 1937 (aged 76) Chicago, Illinois	
Batted: Unknown	**Threw:** Unknown
MLB debut	
June 21, 1879, for the Providence Grays	
Last MLB appearance	
June 21, 1879, for the Providence Grays	
MLB statistics	
Games played	1
Runs	1
Hits	1
Teams	
▪ Providence Grays (1879)	

William Edward White, seated second from right, with the 1879 Brown University varsity baseball team

Very little is known about White, who replaced the regular first baseman, Joe Start, after the latter was injured. White was a student at Brown University, and played for the college's team. He went 1-for-4 and scored a run as Providence won 5–3. It is unknown why White did not play for the Grays again. He was replaced in the next game by future Hall of Famer "Orator Jim" O'Rourke.[7]

SABR's research indicates that the William Edward White who took the field that day was the son of a plantation owner from Milner, Georgia, Andrew Jackson White, and his black slave, Hannah. University records give Milner as the student's birthplace, and the only person of his name listed in the 1870 census was a 9-year-old mulatto boy who was one of three children living with his mother Hannah. All three of these children are named in A.J. White's 1877 will, which described them as the children of his servant Hannah White and stipulated that they be educated in the North. If the research by SABR is correct, then William White was not only the first black player in the major leagues, but may also have been the only former slave.[8][9] Unlike the Walker brothers, White passed as white and did not face the virulent racism prevalent in the late 19th century.

According to 1900 and 1910 census records, White moved to Chicago and became a bookkeeper. He is listed there as having been born in Rhode Island and being white. The 1920 census, however, indicates that there was then a 60-year-old William E. White living in Chicago, whose parents were born in Georgia, and whose race was listed as "black." It is not certain that this is the same man.[10]

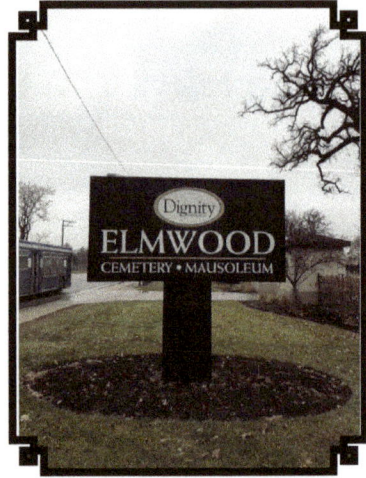

Alvin Strane, author of *The Jersey* and former Minor League Professional Baseball Player of the Seattle Pilots and Milwaukee Brewers, pays his respect to the burial site of the first black Baseball Player, *William E. White* and his father Andrew J. White.

Year Team	Games	BA	SA	AB	H	2B	3B	HR	HR%	R	RBI	BB	SO	SB	Pinch Hit AB	Pinch Hit H	PO	A	E	DP	TC/G	FA	G by Pos

Lou Whitaker *continued*

Year Team	Games	BA	SA	AB	H	2B	3B	HR	HR%	R	RBI	BB	SO	SB	AB	H	PO	A	E	DP	TC/G	FA	G by Pos
1987	5	.176	.353	17	3	0	0	1	5.9	4	1	7	3	1	0	0	11	14	0	1	5.0	1.000	2B-5
2 yrs.	8	.161	.258	31	5	0	0	1	3.2	7	1	7	6	1	0	0	16	20	0	1	4.5	1.000	2B-8

WORLD SERIES

| 1984 DET A | 5 | .278 | .389 | 18 | 5 | 2 | 0 | 0 | 0.0 | 6 | 0 | 4 | 4 | 0 | 0 | 0 | 15 | 18 | 0 | 2 | 6.6 | 1.000 | 2B-5 |

Steve Whitaker

WHITAKER, STEPHEN EDWARD
B. May 7, 1943, Tacoma, Wash.

BL TR 6'   180 lbs.

Year Team	Games	BA	SA	AB	H	2B	3B	HR	HR%	R	RBI	BB	SO	SB	AB	H	PO	A	E	DP	TC/G	FA	G by Pos
1966 NY A	31	.246	.491	114	28	3	2	7	6.1	15	15	9	24	0	0	0	61	3	3	0	2.2	.955	OF-31
1967	122	.243	.358	441	107	12	3	11	2.5	37	50	23	89	2	10	4	202	12	4	6	1.8	.982	OF-114
1968	28	.117	.150	60	7	2	0	0	0.0	3	3	8	18	0	13	2	20	2	2	0	0.9	.917	OF-14
1969 SEA A	69	.250	.440	116	29	2	1	6	5.2	15	13	12	29	2	25	5	45	5	2	0	0.8	.962	OF-39
1970 SF N	16	.111	.148	27	3	1	0	0	0.0	3	4	2	14	0	6	2	6	0	1	0	0.4	.857	OF-9
5 yrs.	266	.230	.367	758	174	20	6	24	3.2	73	85	54	174	4	54	13	334	22	12	6	1.4	.967	OF-207

Bill White

WHITE, WILLIAM BARNEY
B. June 25, 1923, Paris, Tex.

BR TR 5'11"   186 lbs.

| 1945 BKN N | 4 | .000 | .000 | 1 | 0 | 0 | 0 | 0 | 0.0 | 2 | 0 | 1 | 1 | 0 | 0 | 0 | 1 | 1 | 0 | 0 | 0.5 | 1.000 | SS-1 |

Bill White

WHITE, WILLIAM DeKOVA
B. Jan. 28, 1934, Lakewood, Fla.

BL TL 6'   185 lbs.

Year Team	Games	BA	SA	AB	H	2B	3B	HR	HR%	R	RBI	BB	SO	SB	AB	H	PO	A	E	DP	TC/G	FA	G by Pos
1956 NY N	138	.256	.459	508	130	23	7	22	4.3	63	59	47	72	15	0	0	1256	111	15	106	10.0	.989	1B-138, OF-2
1958 SF N	26	.241	.379	29	7	1	0	1	3.4	5	4	7	5	1	16	4	19	1	0	2	0.8	1.000	1B-3, OF-2
1959 STL N	138	.302	.470	517	156	33	9	12	2.3	77	72	34	61	15	5	1	579	27	9	33	4.5	.985	OF-92, 1B-71
1960	144	.283	.455	554	157	27	10	16	2.9	81	79	42	83	12	3	0	1058	66	13	109	7.9	.989	1B-123, OF-29
1961	153	.286	.472	591	169	28	11	20	3.4	89	90	64	84	8	3	0	1373	104	17	125	9.8	.989	1B-151
1962	159	.324	.482	614	199	31	3	20	3.3	93	102	58	69	9	1	0	1260	97	10	116	8.6	.993	1B-146, OF-27
1963	162	.304	.491	658	200	26	8	27	4.1	106	109	59	100	10	0	0	1389	105	13	126	9.3	.991	1B-162
1964	160	.303	.474	631	191	37	4	21	3.3	92	102	52	103	7	0	0	1513	101	6	125	10.1	.996	1B-160
1965	148	.289	.481	543	157	26	3	24	4.4	82	73	63	86	3	4	1	1308	109	11	114	9.6	.992	1B-144
1966 PHI N	159	.276	.451	577	159	23	6	22	3.8	85	103	68	109	16	4	0	1422	109	9	118	9.7	.994	1B-158
1967	110	.250	.360	308	77	6	2	8	2.6	29	33	52	61	6	14	0	775	52	6	85	7.6	.993	1B-95
1968	127	.239	.361	385	92	16	2	9	2.3	34	40	39	79	0	20	5	982	77	6	94	8.4	.994	1B-111
1969 STL N	49	.211	.228	57	12	1	0	0	0.0	7	4	11	15	1	31	5	81	7	0	7	1.8	1.000	1B-15
13 yrs.	1673	.286	.455	5972	1706	278	65	202	3.4	843	870	596	927	103	101	16	13015	966	115	1160	8.4	.992	1B-1477, OF-152

WORLD SERIES

| 1964 STL N | 7 | .111 | .148 | 27 | 3 | 1 | 0 | 0 | 0.0 | 2 | 2 | 2 | 6 | 1 | 0 | 0 | 62 | 3 | 0 | 4 | 9.3 | 1.000 | 1B-7 |

Bill White

WHITE, WILLIAM DIGHTON
B. May 1, 1860, Bridgeport, Ohio D. Dec. 31, 1924, Bellaire, Ohio

Year Team	Games	BA	SA	AB	H	2B	3B	HR	HR%	R	RBI	BB	SO	SB	AB	H	PO	A	E	DP	TC/G	FA	G by Pos
1884 PIT AA	74	.227	.320	291	66	7	10	0	0.0	25		13			0	0	75	206	69	14	4.7	.803	SS-60, 3B-10, OF-4
1886 LOU AA	135	.257	.329	557	143	17	10	1	0.2	96		37			0	0	212	431	96	48	5.5	.870	SS-135, P-1
1887	132	.252	.313	512	129	7	9	2	0.4	85		47		41	0	0	204	431	96	45	5.5	.869	SS-132
1888 2 teams		LOU AA (49G – .278)			STL AA (76G – .175)																		
" total	125	.218	.286	473	103	8	3	0	0.6	66	60	28		21	0	0	199	368	86	16	5.2	.868	SS-112, 3B-11, 2B-2
4 yrs.	466	.241	.312	1833	441	39	37	6	0.3	272	60	125		62	0	0	690	1436	347	123	5.3	.860	SS-439, 3B-21, OF-4, 2B-2, P-1

Bill White

WHITE, WILLIAM EDWARD
B. Milner, Ga. Deceased.

| 1879 PRO N | 1 | .250 | .250 | 4 | 1 | 0 | 0 | 0 | 0.0 | 1 | 0 | 0 | 1 | | 0 | 0 | 12 | 0 | 0 | 1 | 12.0 | 1.000 | 1B-1 |

C. B. White

WHITE, C. B.
B. Wakeman, Ohio Deceased.

| 1883 PHI N | 1 | .000 | .000 | 1 | 0 | 0 | 0 | 0 | 0.0 | 0 | | 0 | 0 | | 0 | 0 | 3 | 1 | 1 | 0 | 5.0 | .800 | SS-1, 3B-1 |

Charlie White

WHITE, CHARLES
B. Aug. 12, 1928, Kinston, N. C.

BL TR 5'11"   192 lbs.

Year Team	Games	BA	SA	AB	H	2B	3B	HR	HR%	R	RBI	BB	SO	SB	AB	H	PO	A	E	DP	TC/G	FA	G by Pos
1954 MIL N	50	.237	.312	93	22	4	0	1	1.1	14	8	9	8	0	24	4	101	4	2	0	2.1	.981	C-28
1955	12	.233	.267	30	7	1	0	0	0.0	3	4	5	7	0	1	0	39	2	0	0	3.4	1.000	C-10
2 yrs.	62	.236	.301	123	29	5	0	1	0.8	17	12	14	15	0	25	4	140	6	2	0	2.4	.986	C-38

Deacon White

WHITE, JAMES LAURIE
Brother of Will White.
B. Dec. 7, 1847, Caton, N. Y. D. July 7, 1939, Aurora, Ill.
Manager 1872, 1879.

BL TR 5'11"   175 lbs.

Year Team	Games	BA	SA	AB	H	2B	3B	HR	HR%	R	RBI	BB	SO	SB	AB	H	PO	A	E	DP	TC/G	FA	G by Pos
1876 CHI N	66	.343	.419	303	104	18	1	1	0.3	66	60	7	3		0	0	318	51	69	3	6.6	.842	C-65, OF-3, 1B-3, 3B-1, P-1
1877 BOS N	59	.387	.545	266	103	14	11	2	0.8	51	49	8	3		0	0	384	22	24	16	7.3	.944	1B-35, OF-19, C-7
1878 CIN N	61	.314	.337	258	81	4	1	0	0.0	41	29	10	5		0	0	277	71	39	4	6.3	.899	C-48, OF-16, 3B-1
1879	78	.330	.423	333	110	16	6	1	0.3	55	52	6	9		0	0	349	96	55	3	6.4	.890	C-59, OF-21, 1B-2
1880	35	.298	.355	141	42	4	2	0	0.0	21	7	9	7		0	0	59	9	17	3	2.4	.800	OF-33, 1B-3, 2B-1
1881 BUF N	78	.310	.411	319	99	24	4	0	0.0	58	53	9	8		0	0	371	119	70	24	7.2	.875	1B-26, 2B-25, OF-17, 3B-7, C-4
1882	83	.282	.341	337	95	17	0	1	0.3	51		15	16		0	0	173	150	55	8	4.6	.854	3B-60, C-20
1883	94	.292	.353	391	114	14	5	0	0.0	62		23	18		0	0	163	165	67	11	4.4	.839	3B-77, C-22
1884	110	.325	.442	452	147	16	11	5	1.1	82		32	13		0	0	130	203	66	19	3.6	.835	3B-108, C-3
1885	98	.292	.337	404	118	6	6	0	0.0	54	57	12	11		0	0	118	198	40	12	3.6	.888	3B-98
1886 DET N	124	.289	.354	491	142	19	5	1	0.2	65	76	31	35		0	0	131	245	68	18	3.6	.847	3B-124
1887	111	.303	.416	449	136	20	11	3	0.7	71	75	26	15	20	0	0	152	227	65	19	4.0	.854	3B-106, OF-3, 1B-2

Sources

1. William Edward White: Statistics and History (https://www.baseball-reference.com/players/w/white bi01.shtml) *Baseball-Reference*
2. Husman, John. "June 21, 1879: The cameo of William Edward White" (http://www.sabr.org/games proj/game/june-21-1879-cameo-william-edward-white). *The Society for American Baseball Research.*
3. Morris, Peter (February 5, 2015). " "Baseball's Secret Pioneer: William Edward White, the first black player in major-league history" " (http://sabr.org/latest/baseballs-secret-pioneer-william-edwa rd-white). *The Society for American Baseball Research/Slate.com.*
4. Malinowski, Zachary (February 15, 2004). "Who was the first black man to play in the major leagues?" (http://www.projo.com). *Providence Journal.*
5. Siegel, Robert (January 30, 2004). "Black Baseball Pioneer William White's 1879 Game" (https:// www.npr.org/templates/story/story.php?storyId=1626450). *National Public Radio.*
6. Fatsis, Stefan (January 30, 2004). "Mystery of Baseball: Was William White Game's First Black?" (https://www.wsj.com/articles/SB107541676333815810). *The Wall Street Journal.*
7. "Was William Edward White really first?" (http://sports.espn.go.com/espn/print?id=1723322&type= story). *Associated Press.* January 30, 2004.
8. Husman, John. "June 21, 1879: The cameo of William Edward White" (http://www.sabr.org/games proj/game/june-21-1879-cameo-william-edward-white). *The Society for American Baseball Research.*
9. Malinowski, Zachary (February 15, 2004). "Who was the first black man to play in the major leagues?" (http://www.projo.com). *Providence Journal.*
10. Siegel, Robert (January 30, 2004). "Black Baseball Pioneer William White's 1879 Game" (https:// www.npr.org/templates/story/story.php?storyId=1626450). *National Public Radio.*

Retrieved from "https://en.wikipedia.org/w/index.php?title=William_Edward_White&oldid=856114451"

This page was last edited on 23 August 2018, at 00:08 (UTC).

American Legion Baseball 1966

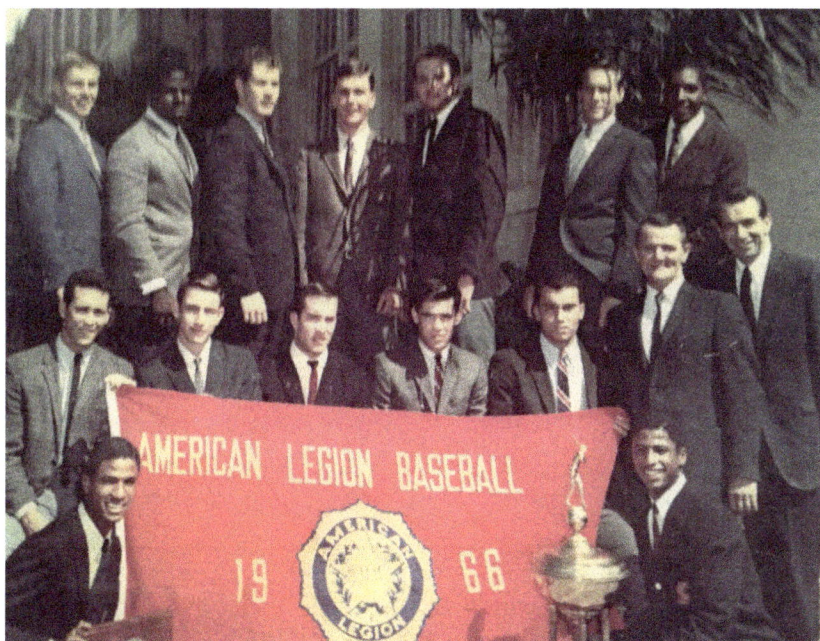

Top Row L-R, Steve Brye, Stanley Williams, Tom Brown, Lynn Adams(RIP), Mick Babler, Phil Williams, Bill Ramsey(RIP)

Middle Row L-R, Paul Brown, Hudson Winslow, Mike Hazelhofer, Terry Adami, Butch Vargus(RIP), Coach Ken Klevin(RIP), Sponsor Sam Bercovich(RIP), Not Pictured Manager Bill Cox(RIP)

Bottom Row L-R, Albert Strane, Al Strane

Rest in Peace, William E. White

www.ingramcontent.com/pod-product-compliance
Lightning Source LLC
Chambersburg PA
CBHW050012090426
42733CB00018B/2642